Three Poets

in conversation

Dick Davis
Rachel Hadas
Timothy Steele

Three Poets
in conversation

Dick Davis
Rachel Hadas
Timothy Steele

BETWEEN THE LINES **BTL** BETWEEN THE LINES

First published in 2006 by

BETWEEN THE LINES **BTL** BETWEEN THE LINES

9 Woodstock Road, London N4 3ET, UK

T :+44 (0)20 8374 5526 F :+44 (0)20 8374 5736 E-mail : btluk@aol.com
Website: http://www.interviews-with-poets.com

The Conversations

copyright © 2006 by Dick Davis and Clive Wilmer

copyright © 2006 by Rachel Hadas and Isaac Cates

copyright © 2006 by Timothy Steele and Cynthia Haven

Editorial Matter

copyright © 2006 by Between The Lines

All rights reserved

A CIP catalogue record for this book is available from the British Library

ISBN 10: 1-903291-14-3

ISBN 13: 978-1-903291-14-6

Design and typography: Philip Hoy

Printed and bound by RPM Print & Design
Chichester, West Sussex, PO19 8PR

BETWEEN THE LINES  BETWEEN THE LINES

EDITORIAL BOARD
Peter Dale Philip Hoy J. D. McClatchy

EDITORIAL ASSISTANT
Ryan Roberts

BTL publishes unusually wide-ranging and unusually deep-going interviews with some of today's most accomplished poets.

Some would deny that any useful purpose is served by putting to a writer questions which are not answered by his or her books. For them, what Yeats called 'the bundle of accident and incoherence that sits down to breakfast' is best left alone, not asked to interrupt its cornflakes, or to set aside its morning paper, while someone with a tape recorder inquires about its life, habits and attitudes.

If we do not share this view, it is not because we endorse Sainte-Beuve's dictum, *tel arbre, tel fruit* — *as the tree, so the fruit* — but because we understand what Geoffrey Braithwaite was getting at when the author of *Flaubert's Parrot* had him say:

> But if you love a writer, if you depend upon the drip-feed of his intelligence, if you want to pursue him and find him – despite edicts to the contrary – then it's impossible to know too much.

Our first thirteen volumes (details of which are given overleaf) were each devoted to a single poet, the youngest of whom was born in 1938. This, our fourteenth volume, represents a new departure, featuring, as it does, three poets, the oldest of whom was born in 1945.

As well as the interview, each volume contains a sketch of the poet's life and career and a bibliography. Some also include a gathering of critical quotations and a gallery of photographs. It is hoped that the results will be of interest to the lay reader and specialist alike.

— Other volumes from BTL —

W.D. Snodgrass
in conversation with
Philip Hoy

Michael Hamburger
in conversation with
Peter Dale

Anthony Thwaite
in conversation with
Peter Dale and Ian Hamilton

Anthony Hecht
in conversation with
Philip Hoy

Donald Hall
in conversation with
Ian Hamilton

Thom Gunn
in conversation with
James Campbell

Richard Wilbur
in conversation with
Peter Dale

Seamus Heaney
in conversation with
Karl Miller

Donald Justice
in conversation with
Philip Hoy

Ian Hamilton
in conversation with
Dan Jacobson

Charles Simic
in conversation with
Michael Hulse

John Ashbery
in conversation with
Mark Ford

Peter Dale
in conversation with
Cynthia Haven

Contents

A photograph of Dick Davis 8
A note on Dick Davis 9
A note on Clive Wilmer 11
Dick Davis in conversation with Clive Wilmer 13

A photograph of Rachel Hadas 44
A note on Rachel Hadas 45
A note on Isaac Cates 47
Rachel Hadas in conversation with Isaac Cates 49

A photograph of Timothy Steele 92
A note on Timothy Steele 93
A note on Cynthia Haven 95
Timothy Steele in conversation with Cynthia Haven 97

Select Bibliographies

    (i)   Dick Davis 143
    (ii) Rachel Hadas 147
    (iii) Timothy Steele 149

Dick Davis

photo courtesy of
Mohammad Batmanglij

A NOTE ON DICK DAVIS

Dick Davis was born in Portsmouth, England, in 1945, and educated at the universities of Cambridge (where he received a BA and an MA in English Literature) and Manchester (where he received a PhD in Medieval Persian Literature). He has taught at the universities of Tehran, Durham, Newcastle, and California, Santa Barbara. Currently he is Professor of Persian and Chair of the Department of Near Eastern Languages and Cultures at Ohio State University.

He lived for eight years in Iran, as well as for periods in Greece and Italy. During his time in Iran he met Afkham Darbandi and they married in 1974. They have two daughters, Mariam, born in 1982, and Mehri, born in 1984.

From about 1978 to 1984 Davis worked as a freelance writer and, during this period, published around a hundred and fifty articles and reviews in the British national press. As author, translator or editor, he has produced twenty-one books. In addition to his academic works he has published translations from Italian prose and from both prose and verse in Persian, not to mention his own books of poetry.

Davis has received a number of awards and honours. In 1979, he received an award from The Arts Council of Great Britain to write a book on Yvor Winters. He was elected a Fellow of the Royal Society of Literature in 1981. In the same year he received an award from The British Institute of Persian Studies to translate Attar's *Manteq alTayr*. Also in this year he received for his book of poems, *Seeing the World*, the Heinemann Award for 'a work of outstanding literary merit'.

He was given a two-year scholarship from the University of Manchester to conduct research on the *Shahnameh* of Ferdowsi and this study led to the PhD mentioned above. During 1987-88 he had a Fulbright Travel Scholarship at the University of California, Santa Barbara.

His selected poems, *Devices and Desires: New and Selected Poems 1967-1987* was chosen by both *The Times* and *The Daily Telegraph* as a Book of the Year in 1989. In this year he was also given a grant in aid of publication award from The Persian Heritage Foundation for *Epic and Sedition: the Case of Ferdowsi's Shahnameh*. In 1993 he received an Ingram Merrill Prize for 'excellence in poetry' for *A Kind of Love*, the revised and expanded US edition of *Devices and Desires*. The Poetry Society of Great Britain awarded him a recommendation for translation for *Medieval Persian Epigrams*, which appeared in 1995. He was a Guggenheim Fellow for 1999-2000. The American Institute of Iranian Studies awarded him its Translation Prize for *My Uncle Napoleon* in 2000. These honours were followed by the *Encyclopaedia Iranica* Prize for Services to Persian Poetry in 2001, the year The American Institute of Iranian Studies again awarded him a translation prize, this time shared with his wife Afkham Darbandi, for *The Conference of the Birds*. His work, in 2002, to translate Volume III of stories from the *Shahnameh* of Ferdowsi, was supported by the National Endowment for the Humanities Award. His book of verse, *Belonging,* was chosen as a Book of the Year in *The Economist,* in 2002.

As a poet, an early passion of Davis's – and one that has not been lost – was for Edward Fitzgerald's *Rubáiyát of Omar Khayyám*. He uses the Fitzgerald stanza in 'A Letter to Omar', a homage to the poet, published in *Devices and Desires*. In fact, he went on to edit a new edition, published in 1989. Such an enthusiasm must have influenced his preference for the expressive qualities of traditional forms and metres that characterize his verse. In his first collection, *In the Distance,* he uses metre and rhyme not in a narrowly old-fashioned formal way but develops with them well-made thoughtful poems that move with a quietly spoken but effective perception. His second book of verse, *Seeing the World*, as mentioned above, received the Royal Society of Literature Award in 1981. *The Covenant* was published in 1984. *Touchwood: Poems 1991-1994* appeared in 1996, along with *Borrowed Ware: Medieval Persian Epigrams,* a verse translation and scholarly edition with introduction and head-notes. *Belonging* appeared in the US and then in the UK in 2002, and Richard Wilbur wrote of it: 'I began by jotting down the titles of the best poems, but gave that up when it seemed I might choose them all.' Davis's most recent collection, published in July 2006, is *A Trick of Sunlight*, which *Booklist's* reviewer called 'one of the most rereadable books of poems of recent years'.

A NOTE ON CLIVE WILMER

Clive Wilmer was born Harrogate in 1945, grew up in London, and was educated at King's College, Cambridge. He now teaches English at Cambridge, where he is a Fellow of Sidney Sussex College, a Bye-Fellow of Fitzwilliam College, and an Honorary Fellow of Anglia Polytechnic University.

He has published seven books of poetry: *The Dwelling-Place* (Carcanet, 1977), *Devotions* (Carcanet, 1982), *Of Earthly Paradise* (Carcanet, 1992), *Selected Poems* (Carcanet, 1995), *The Falls* (Worple Press, 2000), *Stigmata* (Worple, 2005) and *The Mystery of Things* (Carcanet, 2006).

Wilmer is an authority on John Ruskin and his contemporaries, having edited Penguin Classics selections of Ruskin and William Morris and a Carcanet/Fyfield volume of Dante Gabriel Rossetti. He is also a Director of Ruskin's charity, the Guild of St George.

Wilmer has edited essay collections by Thom Gunn and Donald Davie and, in 1985, he conceived and helped organise the Ezra Pound centenary exhibition *Pound's Artists* at the Tate Gallery. With Charles Moseley he edited the anthology *Cambridge Observed* for Colt Books. With George Gömöri, he has translated widely from modern Hungarian poetry, notably the work of Miklós Radnóti and György Petri, and has recently been awarded the annual Pro Cultura Hungarica medal for translation by the Hungarian Ministry of Culture. An occasional broadcaster, he fronted BBC Radio 3's *Poet of the Month* programmes and his interviews from that series are published as *Poets Talking* by Carcanet. He was a founder-editor of the magazine *Numbers* and is a frequent contributor to the *Times Literary Supplement*, *PN Review* and other journals.

DICK DAVIS IN CONVERSATION WITH CLIVE WILMER

More than thirty years ago, you wrote a poem called 'The Epic Scholar', which draws a connection between the matter of epic and the dreams of the solitary thinker who contemplates that matter. You couldn't have known then that you would yourself become such a scholar, one of the world's leading authorities on the Shahnameh *of Ferdowsi, the Persian national epic. Many poets today earn their livings as academics, but I wonder if in your case there isn't some deeper connection between your academic role and your literary one?*

Yes, it is an irony that I should turn into a scholar of epic, having written that poem all those years ago, which rather makes fun of such people; even if quite affectionate, complicit fun. Thus the whirligig of time brings in his revenges. On one level I suppose I was trying for something like Yeats's poem, 'The Scholars', on the editors of Catullus, which is more or less wholly contemptuous of the scholars, and sets up an irritated, neat Life-Scholarship dichotomy. (You can have one or the other, not both). But even when I wrote it I'm pretty sure it was also about how the scholarly life can come from the most atavistic sources, and so be its own version of authenticity. That I still believe to be true: in fact I could say that when I wrote the poem I was guessing it was true. Now I feel I know it to be so. But then the poem is also about living one kind of life and longing for another, and there's a kind of self-mocking humour there because we feel we know very well that most scholars of epic wouldn't last a day if they were somehow magically set down in the kind of society the texts they study were written out of. Certainly when I wrote the poem it never occurred to me that I'd actually finish up as someone who writes about epic, and spends a great deal of time thinking about it.

As for poets earning their living as academics, I'm not so sure that the two avocations do in fact mix so well. In the English-speaking world teaching in an English department has replaced being a country parson as the fallback way of making a living for poets. And it's not all that different an occupation: you're expected to have some learning, to publish a bit, to have a kind of care for people's souls. But one adopts the rhetoric of one's profession, and the general run of the rhetoric of the Humanities in universities now is smugly and depressingly obscurantist and conformist (no tenure if you don't use the approved jargon). It's the kind of stuff that would have made Orwell sick to his stomach, and certainly that can't be good for poetry. There are huge exceptions of course, people able to evade all that, and there are a number of poets I admire who make their living via the academy – Edgar Bowers did, for example, and so did Thom Gunn, and Tim Steele does. Mind you Edgar had deep reservations about the academy, and he didn't get on very well with most academics; and Gunn's relationship to it was rather tangential. I perhaps have something of that tangential quality too, tangential to the business of poetry in the academy anyway, in that I'm not in an English department. The department I teach in is one of Near Eastern Languages and Cultures, and my academic field is medieval Persian. It's interesting that very few of the young poets I admire in the US have anything to do with the academy, or if they do it's not with English departments. And those of my age whose poetry I like are often not in English either: Emily Grosholz is a good example – she teaches philosophy and the history of mathematics. I suppose I'm saying that to write interesting poetry in English it's good, perhaps necessary, to have something else in one's intellectual life, a whole other perspective. Generally the folks that I get on with best in university English departments are medievalists. I know that my academic work on Persian medieval verse feeds my own poetry, but it does so in rather obscure ways (apart from the obvious occasional bits of subject matter). For example, I think I learnt how to write verse narratives largely from reading and translating Persian: there's no better way of seeing how a text is put together than to translate it. Then I find the formal intricacies of medieval Persian verse very beguiling, and something of that has certainly rubbed off on my own practice. But I think it's mainly, and less obviously, to do with my mind being pretty constantly preoccupied by something that is not me, that's very different from me in fact, and that is not here and now, not mired in the contemporary: it's a way out of solipsism, which is one of the great dangers for modern poets.

Even earlier – if I may pursue this line of thought a little further – you wrote a poem called 'Columbus to any Court' – also about a solitary dreamer, though this time a man of action as well. You're a British citizen but you live in the continent Columbus discovered. Is this also relevant to your writing?

There's a poem I'd hoped the mists of time had obscured! It wasn't very good, and that's a generous judgement of it. But it's interesting and strange for me that in those two poems, written just out of my teens I think, I did unwittingly foretell some of my own future, because yes I have become a scholar of epic, and yes I have lived in America for over seventeen years now. That's certainly relevant for my writing in that it has made me see things rather differently, much more nuancedly I'd say, from how I did as a child and adolescent. I like America very much, and the knee-jerk anti-Americanism of many *bien pensant* Europeans rather irritates me. I think it's partly ignorance, but mostly envy, conscious or unconscious. Also the fact that America had to intervene to save Europe from its own genocidal / suicidal impulses three times in the twentieth century (the two world wars and the break up of Yugoslavia) irritates a lot of Europeans. That doesn't mean I like absolutely everything about present-day America of course (I could drone on in very predictable ways about the health-care system here, or the gun laws if you wanted me to), but I often find myself mentally more at home, and in agreement with, American liberals than with many European and British liberals (allowing for the fact that the word has slightly different meanings on either side of the Atlantic). I'd say that America is still a more genuinely open, tolerant and self-critical society, despite all one can say on the other side, than any European or Asian country I'm aware of. Certainly, for me, it's much more so than Britain is or ever has been. Also, although I know it's very unfashionable, even in America itself, to say so, I think they have in general acted more responsibly as top dog than other nations have done in the past. Than Britain did in the nineteenth century, for example. The recent emphatic tilt towards overtly interventionist foreign policy (i.e invasions) in Asia, and the US's at the moment really disastrous relationship with much of the Moslem world, are pretty frightening; but as the world's only current superpower America finds itself damned if it doesn't intervene (Rwanda) and damned if it does (Iraq). On a personal level, in my own experience, a high percentage of educated Americans are very nice people indeed: to begin with they tend to lack the innate sense of superiority that educated Europeans often have. They don't automatically adopt a *de haut en bas* attitude towards the rest of the world. In a word, they're democrats. Of course uneducated Americans can be a pain in the neck, and a terrifying pain in the neck at that, but that can be true of uneducated people anywhere. A mob is a mob – American, British, French, Chinese or Iranian. It's true that there are many things to be said in favour of the European shores of the Atlantic. For example, America's beauty is in general natural beauty, which is not something I especially respond to, though I do my best, and even I can see that it is *really* spectacular. But for man-made beauty, artifacts and buildings, which *are* what I especially respond to, the smallest Italian town usually has more interesting and lovely things, man-made things, crowded within ten square miles than a whole state in the US has. I miss that, and find it overwhelming when I go back to Europe. It's like when my wife and I were in Afghanistan and India for four months, and didn't hear any western music at all in that whole time, because we were mostly in rural areas that had little communication with the outside world: then when we got back home we visited a friend who happened to have Brahms's *Alto Rhapsody* on the record player. Now I don't especially like Brahms's music normally, but after that longish absence from western music the *Alto Rhapsody* seemed really astonishingly, heartbreakingly, beautiful, in a kind of revelatory way. That's how Italian or French medieval and renaissance architecture can strike one, or me anyway, after coming from the US. But to respond to how living in America has been relevant to my poetry: it's been so in a couple of ways I think. One is that I have a number of American poet friends now, and many of the twentieth-century poets I most admire are Americans, so I feel continuous with that world in a small way, even though my own poetic accent is obviously a British one. Another is a sense of the would-be egalitarian multiplicity of American society, which constantly produces the kinds of cultural mixing that I often write poems out of. Both those things were present for me before I came to America, but certainly a consciousness of them has deepened since I've been here.

But are you in any sense now an American poet rather than a British one – or does the question make no sense to you?

I think this has to be a question about identity, and one's sense of one's own identity, and these are of course very fluid categories. But poetic identity, though we know it can be, and is, modified by many experiences, has its defining landscapes laid down in childhood surely. Or at least for the great majority of us I'd say that's true. When we think for example of Eliot and Pound, to most of us they seem *echt* American poets, despite their long sojourn in Europe, Eliot's taking British citizenship and receiving the OM, Pound's support for the Italian Fascist Party, and so forth. Similarly Auden and Gunn both seem to me very British poets despite their obvious love of American life. My own poetic dialect, in so far as it exists, is I think wholly British, even if it's sometimes a bit outré in its references and concerns. I think that would still be the case if I were to become a US citizen. It's not something one has much control over. I have a number of American poet friends, and I'm pretty sure they think of me as a British poet who happens to live in the US. I think I'd have to agree with that.

Of course, America is not the only country you know well. You have lived in Greece, Italy and for several years in Iran. You have an Iranian wife. And you have travelled extensively in both Asia and Europe.

Travel itself, just the sheer fact of being on the move from one place to another, was perhaps most important to me in my twenties. I did have very itchy feet then; I was always keen to be elsewhere as soon as possible, and I wrote quite a few poems out of and around that subject matter. Much of my first book, *In the Distance*, is about that. The title virtually announces that that's the main subject matter. But then it became replaced for me by the sensations and complexities of living in a culture that wasn't mine, which isn't at all the same thing, though the two can overlap. There was a very simple analogy for me when I was young I think, which was something like 'travel is a high in itself and it's also a metaphor for the search for a meaning to one's life'. That's a solipsistic enterprise, and I think quintessentially a young person's enterprise, one that also chimed in with a lot that was happening then – I was in my early twenties in the late 1960s – for many young western people interested enough and lucky enough to get out and see something of the world. But as I lived in various places it was quite soon replaced by a search for, and I hope a respect for, the meanings and patterns that other cultures put before me, made available to me. So it became not so much a meaning to my life that I was looking for, as meanings that were 'out there', independent of me, that didn't need me. A number of the poems in my second and third books, *Seeing the World* and *The Covenant*, are about issues like that. And when they're about me in the landscape they're basically about how I don't matter in the landscape, which doesn't need me there. I'd go so far as to say that most of the poems in those two books are basically about that. Finding out that the world is more interesting than oneself. A writer I can hardly read now with any tolerance or sympathy, but one who was very important to me as an adolescent, was D. H. Lawrence, and I still find that of all his writings, most of which, as I say, I can't now stomach, I like and admire his travel writing. Someone wrote that Lawrence was 'a chauvinist of all cultures', or of all cultures that he visited anyway, and I think that was true of me for a while. It isn't now, or not so much. Now, I'm most at home with a kind of transcultural sympathy. I'm not so interested in cultural authenticity as I was – whatever cultural authenticity is (and whatever it is, it unfortunately often seems to end up in involving cultural parochialism and prejudice); I care more about the blurring of cultural boundaries, and what happens at that moment of blurring and subsequently. That preoccupation is there from *Seeing the World* on (which came out in 1980) in a poem like 'Syncretic and Sectarian', about the Moghul Prince Dara Shukoh and his brother Aurungzeb. Dara Shukoh was a fascinating individual; a Moslem prince whose spiritual guide was a Jewish convert to Sufism and who translated the Upanishads into Persian. He clearly had a mind that relished the points at which cultures and world-views can touch and interact. He was the heir apparent to the Moghul empire, but before he could inherit the throne was defeated in battle by his younger brother, Aurungzeb, who became the most intransigently inflexible of Moslem rulers, one who seems to have had only contempt for Hinduism. My interest in the kind of cultural reaching out exemplified by Dara Shukoh has strengthened over the years. So, in so far as I can see a journey there, I moved from an interest in travel *per se*, to a concern with specific other cultures, to an interest in the kind of mind that reaches across cultural divides. My poetry charts that general pilgrimage I think. It has been a kind of pilgrimage, if one can have a secular pilgrimage.

You love places of crossed culture. You admire syncretism ...

Oh syncretism, we haven't enough space to get seriously into that. I'm convinced that virtually all cultural progress, if we can use that nebulous word, has happened because of it. But really it's everywhere, just that in some places it's more dramatically visible than others. All modern cultures are irretrievably hybrid, thank God, even when they are most convinced of their purity, and the need to defend it. Aimé Césaire says somewhere that our cultures are heterogeneous but that this heterogeneity is experienced internally as a homogeneity. A small example: I've just received copies of an essay I wrote on the role of verse translation in the development of the rhetoric of English poetry. Virtually every metrical form in English poetry has entered the language because of translation – and so as an act of conscious cultural syncretism. And of course this isn't just true of England, nor is it just true of poetry. When you unpeel a national tradition, taking away what has come from elsewhere, it tends to be like Peer Gynt's onion. The irreducible ethnic core that nationalists so love turns out to be just not there. Nothing is so fascinating as tracing the ways in which cultures get muddled up. Not that the process of their being muddled is always painless. On the contrary, it can sometimes be, as we know, very bloody. But for whatever obscure reasons I feel naturally attracted to and at home with people and artifacts that are obviously products of cultural complexity. I've just recently met someone who was born of Greek parents in the Lebanon, grew up speaking Arabic, was educated in France and England, and is doing a PhD in the American midwest on medieval English philosophy. Can you imagine the cultural resonances banging about in that young man's head? The kind of layered, palimpsest mental landscape such a history implies is really fascinating for me; just thinking about its possibilities is pure joy. One of the reasons I became interested in Persian Sufi poetry was that some forms of it take that kind of intellectual and emotional heterogeneity as a given – the assumption is that the 'pure' life is the unexperienced life. That's not true of all Sufi verse of course, which is very various, and much of it can be as po-faced as the dullest specimens in an Anglican hymnal.

With most people these dreams begin in childhood. One thinks of Baudelaire and 'Le Voyage', which I know you love. How did you start writing verse? And is the poet who wrote your earliest poems still recognizable in the poet who writes your poems now?

I find it difficult to say how and when poetry entered my life, but I know it came early and hard. I cannot remember a time when I didn't read poetry voraciously, and write it, and assume that it would be an important part of my life. My mother liked poetry and read it to me as a child. I remember her reading Wilde's 'The Ballad of Reading Gaol' to me: a rather lugubrious poem to read to a young boy, but I liked it very much, I remember. Probably what I really liked were the attention, and her visible emotion. I can still remember what the first 'grown-up' poems I discovered for myself were, and which moved me – one was by Longfellow, and was about an African slave, the other was Byron's 'The Dying Gaul'. I guess I was about ten or eleven when I found those two poems. Though I didn't realize it then, both, I can now see, had a connection with my later concern with foreign-ness, and with victimized foreign-ness at that, since both are about individuals plucked from their own culture and misused by another. The poems I wrote as a child and an adolescent were of the kind that many children and adolescents write. I was certainly no Rimbaud. I think the first poem I'd still acknowledge without too much shame or embarrassment was written when I was about twenty. There is a continuity between those poems and what I write now, I think, but they were very mawkish of course, and like most adolescents I really had nothing to say that thousands of other adolescents weren't saying: I just had a desire to say something, and to say it effectively. But the themes were not so different from what came later: exploration, a hankering for the vast elsewhere, historical anecdotes. And love poems: awfully bad love poems. I spent much of my adolescence in a delirium of sentimental crushes, and wrote about them *ad nauseam*.

Writing about the earliest poems you published, Tony Tanner, who taught you at Cambridge, talks of you making tokens 'out of the fragments from the vast excavated battlefield which is history'. Reading these early pieces I'm conscious, not only of a concern with history, but even more of a concern with violence, wreckage, destruction and mass killing – the matter of epic again perhaps. Yet most of what you have written in maturity strikes the reader as lucid, orderly and civilized. Is there a continuity?

I'm glad you mentioned Tony. He was a wonderful teacher, and a wonderful man. A real mensch, as Americans say, and endlessly learned and generous with his learning. I've been extraordinarily lucky with three of my teachers: my secondary school English teacher, John Gibson, who I'm pleased to say is still a friend of mine, Tony at Cambridge, and later on Edgar Bowers, whom I sought out because I admired his poetry so much, and who became a kind of avuncular mentor to me. I'm very, very grateful to all three of them. Concerning the violent early poems and the, as you put it lucid, civilized later ones. There is for me an obvious connection, which is I suppose that violence and cruelty are the nature of human life and history except for during those too short lucid intervals when reason and civilized values prevail. When you and I were children, Clive, the culture was soaked in the just-over reality of World War II, and especially the revelation of the concentration camps. I brooded about all that in my adolescence a lot, as I know many of my generation did. Then there were the revelations about Stalinist Russia. Then a bit later Biafra and Cambodia. Later still Rwanda. But it was probably trying to take on board the concentration camps as an adolescent, and what that did to our expectations of life, that prepared us mentally for all the rest; so that the rest didn't come as that much of a surprise. We knew it all as possible, likely even. The early poems you mention were written out of that. When I was in my early twenties one of my favourite poems was Gunn's poem on the Von Stauffenberg plot on Hitler's life. The last stanza of that, with its wonderful last line, was a model for the kind of poetry I wanted to be able to write then.

> And though he fails, honour personified
> In a cold time where honour cannot grow,
> He stiffens, like a statue, in mid-stride
> – Falling toward history, and under snow.

Also there were things in my own life at that time that made me preternaturally aware of death and mental terror, and they must have contributed. As an adult I have never been remotely attracted by the Rousseauist notion that human instincts are fine and good and that all we need to do is cultivate them properly. History emphatically does not bear out the notion that human instincts are fine and good, and the most terrible revelation of Nazi Germany was perhaps that the worst imaginable things could be done by perfectly ordinary people like you and me. The banality of evil, as Hannah Arendt put it. It seems reasonable to me to want to cultivate lucidity and reason, if one is not just to throw up one's hands in total despair, as a result of that. Anything that keeps the wolves of barbarism at bay is to be encouraged I feel. So for me there is a continuity, though it was almost certainly my own personal circumstances that led me to see and emphasize the darkness early on and the lucidity later. Very few of those dark poems are in print now: most of them preceded my first book. And they weren't very good anyway: what can a twenty-year-old say about such things?

Young poets tend to take up subjects and ways of writing for all sorts of fairly unreal reasons – what's fashionable, what, from among the things that are fashionable, might seem to speak to them or their peers most insistently. It all seems so inevitable at the time, and for each individual so from within oneself, but looking back you see that it's merely everyone aping what's around. For me, all that started to change when I left England as soon as I'd graduated from Cambridge, and that pressure – which is very subtle and strong – toward intellectual conformity (the implicit, 'these are the concerns we-in-the-know have this year, these are the books we are reading, these are the démodé things we sneer at …') all began to fall away, and I saw that I just wasn't interested in belonging to what Harold Rosenberg memorably called 'the herd of independent minds'. That was a relief. Still, when I come back to England I can quickly find myself a bit hostage to all that again, and want to rid myself of it as soon as I can.

Are you still someone whose prime concern is history?

Well, professionally I'm a medievalist, and the texts I deal with are mostly about a thousand years old, give or take a hundred years or so. And they're often epic texts: epic is a kind of mythologising of history. That's certainly a concern with history. A lot of the subjects of my poems are still taken from history. But it's true that there is much less a sense of 'history is a nightmare from which I am trying to wake up' about many of my recent poems. I've seen, I guess, that history contains much that is benign and beguiling as well as horrific. And – this may sound very naïve but so be it – I have begun in my middle age really to value happiness, and to feel that it should be pushed along and promoted whenever and wherever that's possible. God knows there's enough of its opposite about. I guess when you're young you feel 'Why don't people realize how appalling life has been for most people at most times?', so you write about that. Later on you take that appallingness as a given, and look for light where it's findable. It could be America you know. America is very into happiness. It's in the Declaration of Independence, and it's taken seriously as a goal. And I don't think I want to be sniffily European or British about that.

Was Cambridge important to you?

Very, though I hardly realized it at the time. I came up as a gauche, shy, lower middle class eighteen year old from a rural state school in East Yorkshire, to King's, which was still a fairly aristocratic college then, even though I arrived at the time that that was changing. I was pretty out of place, if not wholly alone in my out-of-placeness. Also things were falling apart in my own family for all the time I was up, and my brother killed himself during my final year as an undergraduate. Before he did so I was for quite a while preoccupied with looking after him, finding care for him and so forth, as he was quite ill. So one might think I wasn't really in a position to benefit from what Cambridge had to offer. Also I was quite unhappy, and though I can now see clearly enough that that wasn't at all Cambridge's fault, my position there as a quasi-outsider encouraged me to think that it might be at least partially Cambridge's fault. But despite all this I got an immense amount from those rather miserable three years. Tony Tanner was my supervisor; he was a great teacher (and I'm not using the word 'great' loosely), he was very kind to me, and he encouraged me to write poetry after I had shown him some adolescent verses. The first poem I ever had published was due to his sending it off to an American journal, *TriQuarterly*, without telling me he'd done so (I guess he didn't tell me so that I wouldn't be disappointed if they turned it down). And I had many other very good teachers as well as him. Also E.M. Forster was a presence in the college then, and though I never got to know him well I did get to know him a bit (I still have a couple of short letters he wrote to me) and I find that I revere his memory. If I had to point to one piece of writing that encapsulates what I feel about how we should conduct our lives it would be to his essay 'What I Believe'. I don't think I'd ever have gone to the middle east, or become a specialist in Persian, if it hadn't been for Forster. Also I made friends at that time who are still my closest friends. So yes, against the odds, considering the mess I was in at the time, Cambridge was very important to me. It broadened my intellectual horizons enormously: I don't think it's too much to say that in a way it civilized me, despite all the bad personal and familial stuff that was happening in my life at that time. It offered me a way out of all that. And it was the place where I met other people who were as interested in writing poetry as I was, chief among them being Robert Wells and yourself of course, and the opportunity to have talented friends who are as passionate as you are about something when you are young is a godsend; I think that's probably especially true for people who want to create things – poets or painters or musicians. It helped me immensely I know. That's a pretty good haul for three years, especially when one remembers that one is actually up for less than half of each year.

I associate you mostly with very short poems. You tend to be sparing of detail and the poem often has a single striking point to make. This is by way of suggesting that you are primarily an epigrammatist.

It's true I do like epigrams, and I do like poems to come to an epigrammatic conclusion when that's appropriate. I like aesthetic closure, and the process of homing in on it. I find it very satisfying, like filling in the last clue in a recalcitrant crossword puzzle, or playing a good end-game in chess. I'm not very good at either crossword puzzles or chess, so for me that aesthetic *frisson* comes mostly from making verses. Poems that work primarily in that kind of a way haven't much vogue now (though one of the greatest practitioners of the form, J.V. Cunningham, was a twentieth century poet). Epigrams have a noble history, of course, going back to the Greek Anthology and beyond. My liking for them is a temperamental thing, I guess. I like clarity and wit, and epigrams are often built on those two qualities. And of course you try to make the kind of poem you enjoy reading. It might seem strange that coupled with this I like long narrative poems, and that my scholarly work is largely taken up with them. What unites the two genres, I think, is, to put it naively and bluntly, a concern with how things are in the world: how things pan out, how lives are formed by circumstance, how arbitrary and (simultaneously) inevitable lives (or characters, or situations) can appear in retrospect. Epigram and epic are escapes from lyric solipsism, which – oh certainly – I can be drawn to as easily as the next romantic, but it's still something I'm very fearful and suspicious of. That concern for the world out there being in a poem is one of the reasons I like pre-seventeenth-century English poetry so much; it's always bumping up against the reality of the world, mediated by a sensibility of course, but not mediated away, not sublimated into something else. I guess that's one reason Chaucer is just about my favourite English poet. Or a seventeenth-century poet like Marvell who seems so conscious of the struggle between the kind of cussed thereness of the world and the mind's temptations to volatilize it into something quite different: that's very heartening and heady for me to read. Too often in later periods you feel the struggle has become lost somewhere, or is thought of as not what poetry does.

When you started writing, the obvious sources were Blake and Dickinson. Then that changed quite suddenly to J. V. Cunningham, Yvor Winters, and the older poets praised by them. How did that happen?

Well, my first conscious models weren't Dickinson and Blake, they were more like Byron and Shelley. But that was when I was thirteen, fourteen years old. I was in a Dickinson and Blake phase (the Blake of *Songs of Experience*) when I went up to Cambridge, and I guess those were the first poems of mine you saw. Dickinson was something of my own discovery, and I was proud of that. She wasn't taught or read much then in England, *no* American poetry was taught then at Cambridge, except unofficially by people like Tony, and though the Thomas Johnson complete edition of her poems had come out by that time it certainly wasn't easily available to a schoolboy in rural Yorkshire. So I was reading the Bianchi /Loomis Todd versions, I guess, but I thought they were terrific. And of course the sensibility was clearly eccentric, and young poets love that. It wasn't such a jump from Dickinson to Cunningham for me – there's a spareness of diction in both, and a preference for the short line, and the tendency to look for epigrammatic conclusions that we've just talked about. Though I agree their sensibilities are quite different, and that's putting it mildly. But I placed them both with Wyatt and Hardy at the time I was an undergraduate, I remember, thinking of them as a loose group who wrote a kind of poetry I'd like to be able to write: verbally spare and psychologically sharp; with a kind of hard stoicism that was embodied in rather spiky, brittle, take-no-prisoners language. Winters I discovered by chance. I picked up a book of his poems in a shop and it fell open at 'The California Oaks', which is an absolutely wonderful poem. I read it and was bowled over, and bought the book. I was nineteen, I think. Then I talked about Winters with Tony, and he told me about Winters's criticism, and also about Gunn's connection with him. Gunn and Tony were good friends, and a little later I met Gunn at a party in Tony's rooms, and I asked him about Winters too. For a while, a couple of years at least, Winters's *Collected Poems* was one of my favourite books. I read the criticism too, because I liked the poems so much, but though I liked it, especially the jokes, it was the poems I really admired. He certainly changed the way I wrote: I stopped trying to use noticeable and eccentric language, I became more conscious of metrical effects, I tried to really make and shape the poems I was writing, instead of just letting them sprawl about. I became hyperconscious of the pentameter line, and what you could do with it. Most of my poems up to that point had been in much shorter lines. But my sensibility is not like his, not at all, and his themes were never mine. It was technique I wanted from him, not a poetic ethos or a set of subjects. Once I had absorbed what Winters was saying about technique it was easy to see how good a poet Bowers was. Years later, when my first book of poems was published, I sent a copy to Bowers with a fan letter, and that's how we became friends. His poetry has meant an incalculable amount to me. I don't think it has literally influenced me much, except in very minor ways perhaps, probably partly because his voice is so distinctive but also because I came to it too late and I wasn't malleable any more in that way. But certainly the seriousness and austerity of his verse, the wonderfully assured and unfussy technique, the readiness to take on great subjects and to address them appropriately, all these have been an admonition to me to write better, not to be lazy, to extend what I'm capable of.

Some people have called you a 'Wintersian'. You have written an excellent critical study of Winters in fact. Do you accept the soubriquet?

Not really: certainly not now and probably not ever. There's too much in my make-up, and in my interests, that's too different from what Winters cared about or could have cared about. Can you imagine Winters getting excited about Persian Sufi poetry? Very unlikely! Also he was contemptuous of epic as a form, and I find epic *really* fascinating: indeed much of my writing on Persian poetry is on epic, as we've mentioned. And Winters was into a kind of purity, I guess: I'm definitely into hybridity. We're both children of our particular time in that of course. But there are many things in his work I find very admirable. I mean apart from the poems, a number of which I still like very much indeed. He was a most marvellous reader, in that he had an uncanny eye for singling out annihilatingly good poems that everyone up to then had missed or passed over. His promotion of the Elizabethan poet Gascoigne's poems, for example, or the sonnets of the New England writers Tuckerman and Jones Very. He was like Geoffrey Grigson in that, though the two of them clearly operated by different criteria, and probably wouldn't have had a lot that was polite to say to one another. Like a number of pretty trenchant critics (Leavis for example) I feel he was much better on what he admired than on what he dismissed, even though I often agree with the dismissals. I guess what I'm most grateful for is that he said it's OK to think, and to think rationally, in a poem; in fact it's good to think in a poem. After all the anti-intellectual, self-indulgent cant of much of late romanticism and then of imagism, and then in Europe of surrealism, that was such a relief. Like a sudden shower of ice-cold spring water after slogging through warm sticky goo for far too long. He traced a persistent tradition of interesting real thought embodied in poetry. Also he showed you how a poem is consciously made, which it is, of course, instead of the poet being completely dependent on a kind of vatic accident. This is not to deny the role of talent or the subconscious or inspiration or whatever we call it, but the role of the shaping conscious mind is crucial. His writings showed me that. And he was not afraid to designate charlatans as such: he did it in a curmudgeonly way that made him enemies (no one ever said he was good fun as company), but I was glad he did it. I never knew him, which was a source of some regret to me, though I doubt we'd have got on very well. I think he'd have found my mind a bit all over the place, if he'd deigned to notice it. My secondary school history teacher once said to me, 'Davis, you'll never come to anything, you have a grasshopper mind'. I do too, and I think Winters would have been dismissive of that, so maybe it's as well we didn't meet. I did get to know his widow, the novelist and poet Janet Lewis, as I know you did too, and like most people who knew her I just adored her. She was a very fine person; wonderfully courteous, wise, kind, everything one longs for in a friend. The closest person to sanctity I've ever known personally I think. Afkham my wife loved her too.

Something you share with Winters and Cunningham is an interest in philosophy. But your thinking, for me, at one time had a dimension one perhaps misses in them. One could call it mystical perhaps, or religious. It's prepared for in your first book, In the Distance *– for instance in a poem called 'Names' – and it plays an important role in your second book,* Seeing the World. *More recently it seems to have departed. Could you reflect a little on the religious and the metaphysical in relation to your poems?*

This is difficult; it's a hard area for me to talk about. Partly, I think, because the Sufis got it right; those things can't be put into words (even though many Sufi poets use an awful lot of words to tell us that. Many of them have real logorrhea). In a fairly recent poem, 'Aubade', I characterized myself as an atheist, and I guess finally that's what I am. But that's partly an irritated and slightly flippant response to living in the midwest. Much as I love America, and I do, one of the things that makes me uncomfortable here is the way, in the midwest at least, a rather simplistic Christianity is so omnipresent. Honk for Jesus. I'd rather shoot myself. To be serious about your question: I'm very moved by sanctity and the idea of sanctity, of someone trying to live a wholly good life. Obviously there could be no better thing to do with your life. But the way religion often manifests itself is not in personal sanctity but in sectarian hatred. I'm in Near Eastern Studies, for God's sake, so it would be hard for me not to notice that. There's a dilemma here that I don't really see a way around, and it's this. Without dogma, religion very quickly becomes mere touchy-feely mush, and one can only have contempt for that. With dogma it very quickly turns into a weapon of really horrifying cruelty. The kind of thing the Israeli movie *Kadosh* documents, when people get so snagged on the interpretation of a 2,000 year old text that they lose all sense of decency and humanity: they cease to be human, as you and I recognize the word. The kind of thing that leads to Khomeini saying it's fine to execute all the political prisoners, or to the Taliban erasing women from public life, or to Protestants stoning Catholic primary school children in Northern Ireland. And you're doing this because you think God tells you to? The mind of someone like me can hardly begin to take that mindset in, but it's everywhere in the modern world, and it's getting worse. So in general I don't feel religion is much of a source for good these days. I do still love sanctity and the idea of it. Someone like Bonhoeffer, or Maximilian Kolbe, or Korczak, who figures in a wonderful poem by Bowers, or the White Rose group, which Catherine Tufariello wrote a really lovely poem about, or Raoul Wallenberg. Those people were all killed, of course, and one can't but bow down before that; one can't but know that one is hopelessly lacking put beside such people. I guess I want secular sanctity, and that is perhaps an impossibility. In poems where I touch on such subjects – I've written an epigram about Kolbe for example – I'm more moved by the practical results, in the world, of someone else's faith, rather than by the faith *per se*. Though I can see well enough that with no faith those people would not have acted in the ways they did, or they'd have been much less likely to anyway. They are moved by God, but it's their being moved that moves us, not the vision that spoke to them. They become the vision for us. I'm drawn to the religious sensibility, as you can see, but I'm also very, *very* suspicious of it, because of the extreme ugliness with which religion often manifests itself in the world. Of course you can say

'That's not real religion', but that's not what the people who are doing the killing and stoning would say. For them it *is* real religion. The world is full of people who in the name of religion say 'We have got it right and everyone else has got it wrong'. From there it's the shortest step, the merest flicker of a zealot's eyebrow, to saying 'And something must be done about everyone else'.

As for metaphysics, well I'm not a metaphysician. Plato says that all philosophy begins in wonder, and I certainly have that, but I don't get much further. I love reading philosophy, in an amateur way, and for a while I thought that Kant was the truth, but of course I don't have the philosophical training or equipment to assess Kant in any real way. I'm nagged at by the questions everyone is intermittently nagged at by, that's all. Like virtually everyone of my generation whom I know, who's even slightly bothered by such things, I've been drawn to Buddhism. I love T. R. V. Murti's book, *The Central Philosophy of Buddhism*, which I first read maybe thirty years ago and still admire. But I'm in no way a Buddhist. Still, the idea of a religion without a God is an attractive one for me. But one can't make a fruit cocktail of religions; that's back to contemptible mush again. There, to say that I can't talk about it I've used almost as many words as a Sufi poet might.

I suppose your discovery of Persian poetry and Sufi philosophy was important here. It's interesting that you've made a speciality of translating Persian epigrams – notably in the book called Borrowed Ware.

I think it's significant that the long Sufi poem Afkham and I translated in the 1980s, Attar's *Conference of the Birds*, is about the *search* for truth, rather than about truth itself. The search, the journey – it's a book about mental travelling – is something I find easier to identify with than with any version of 'the truth itself', though of course Attar does try to characterize that at the end of the book. But he does so in such a poetic, allegorical, and sheerly beautiful way, that one doesn't feel oppressed or excluded by the dogma. Certainly, I won't deny that the Sufi sensibility is one I find very attractive in many of its manifestations. But you notice I haven't translated any Sufi prose, and in fact I've turned down a number of requests to do so, at least one of which would have been very lucrative. Finally, in Sufi poetry, it's the poetry I care about: without the poetry the Sufism itself, for me, is just another unprovable – and, to be honest, I think quite spectacularly unlikely – metaphysical system (or systems, Sufis disagree with one another an awful lot about details). I was drawn to Attar mainly because he is the most marvellous poet, a great, world-class poet, the Persian Dante if you like. I like him even more than Rumi, who is more popular of course. And the epigrams you mention are moments, aperçus, quick insights, so you aren't dealing with a whole metaphysic; they're more a series of snapshots of the soul at brief moments. And, as we said a few minutes ago, I just like epigrams, Sufi or not Sufi.

Have poetries other than English and Persian affected you? I'm thinking perhaps of Greek – a poet like Cavafy?

One of the real regrets of my life is that I was too stupid to try to learn modern Greek thoroughly, or even in any way at all beyond a bare minimum, during the year I lived in Greece. I was just down from Cambridge, and still caught up in that maelstrom of psychological stuff we talked about before. But I should have done, it would have been very good for me, and I'd be able to read Cavafy properly, instead of with a facing text and glancing across the page as I have to do now. Yes, certainly Cavafy has affected me, very strongly I think. In a way, for me, he is the quintessential modern poet, and he's certainly the great poet of conscious cultural hybridity. It's probably true to say that a large number of my poems could never have been written if I hadn't read Cavafy. Not that the influence is so direct or obvious perhaps, but I feel almost wholly at home with his sensibility, and his poems showed me ways to write about the kind of culturally hybrid subject matter that interested him and interests me. 'Syncretic and Sectarian' for example, which is in *Seeing the World*, or 'Fraulein X' in *The Covenant*, or 'A Letter to Omar', from the same book, or 'A Monorhyme for Miscegenation' which is in *Touchwood*, all owe a lot to Cavafy. Not that those poems sound especially like Cavafy, or I don't think they do anyway, but my having read his work was probably a prerequisite of their being written. The other poet I have to read in facing texts, and who has been almost as important for me as Cavafy, is Borges. I know people love the stories and the essays, and I do too (especially the essays), but it's the poems I really care for. That's another sensibility I feel a very strong kinship with, while naturally being in awe of his immense talent, as with Cavafy. After Persian the language I can read most easily in is Italian, and a number of Italian poets have meant a lot to me. I have no original claims to make there – the ones that speak most strongly to me are the usual ones, Dante and Leopardi especially. You mentioned Baudelaire before, who is another poet who has meant a great deal to me. Baudelaire's formal exposition of very recalcitrant subject matter is a wonderful object lesson for a young poet. The other French poet I really, really admire is Ronsard: he gets so much of the world in his poems, and they are so openly charming. Even when they are not about happiness you can feel the happiness of the act of creation, of being a poet, a maker, pulsing in them all the time. That's very beguiling. He's a bit like George Herbert in that way. When I don't know the languages, I read a lot of poetry in translation. You always wonder what you're missing, but often there's enough to keep you fascinated. One of my favourite translations from a language I don't know is your book of Miklós Radnóti's poems, and believe me I'm not just saying that because you're interviewing me. I think it's a wonderful book, and one of the great verse translations to have appeared in my lifetime.

You're thought of as – I hate the word – a 'formalist'. Someone very committed to writing in the traditional forms and metres. Do you accept the description?

Yes, I rather hate the word too, but that's only because it seems redundant to me. Or perhaps better to say that I feel it should be redundant. Certainly I'm not a 'new formalist'. New formalists tended to grow up with free verse and they turned to formal verse as an alternative to free verse. I grew up with formal – I prefer the word metrical – verse and it's what I've always written. I think my flirtation with free verse lasted for all of a month, some time around when I was eighteen. I like metrical verse, I suppose, because its effects are more certain and visible, and quantifiable, than those of free verse. I think of verse primarily as a craft; crafts involve the fulfilment of expectations, and the expectations are clear in metrical verse and usually wholly opaque in free verse (isn't that what free means, that the expectations go out of the window?) And for this reason I have trouble hearing free verse rhythmically, and I think most people do. The evidence for this is that popular verse has always been metrical verse. The most popular verse around at the moment is the lyrics of popular music, virtually all of which rhyme and scan of course, even if only in a minimal way. By the way, it infuriates me when people say that metrical verse is élitist: on the contrary, it is free verse that is élitist, if we are going to throw that word about. Very little free verse has ever had a really popular audience, but enormous amounts of metrical verse have, as witness the song lyrics I just mentioned. I think what's meant by saying that metrical verse is élitist is that some people find it hard to write it in a way that isn't embarrassingly incompetent. But in that case playing any musical instrument or participating in any sport is also élitist. Few of us will play Carnegie Hall, and few of us will play Wimbledon. You have to be really good to do so. Too bad, that's how the world is. But to get back to hearing free verse. It seems to me to be highly arbitrary and unverifiable: there is no way of knowing why it is as it is or how it is to be read. A good example of this happened for me when I read Winters's early free verse poems, which are in very short unpunctuated lines. I had imagined them as to be read very slowly, raptly, intensely, with a long pause at each line-end. Then I heard a recording of Winters reading them: he reads them very fast, rushing through them helter-skelter, with no pause whatsoever at any line-end. Who could know that that was how he heard them? And if it doesn't matter how it's read then I don't see the point of calling it verse at all. But in formal verse the metre tells us, within some margins, how to read the poem, where to pause, where the emphases come, when to build, when to fade, and so forth. As for writing one's own poems, the important thing surely is to do what you care about, to have some integrity and to write out of what you believe in, and to write in the way you find pleasurable, which means in the way you find effective (because such writing affects you, that's why it's pleasurable for you and so you (try to) write in that way). And if others don't share your tastes, well so be it: at least you haven't lied to them or to yourself. There's hardly a single poem in free verse that gives me any pleasure I've realized. I just don't like it, I get no buzz / charge / satisfaction / glow from it. It really is as simple as that for me: it's like not liking Brussels sprouts. Which I don't.

Are you opposed to poetic experiment?

Being opposed to poetic experiment sounds like being opposed to mom and apple pie. No, I'm not opposed: I've done it often enough myself. For example, I have adapted some Persian classical forms to English. But I guess for me, once you abandon metrical repetition, you have abandoned the basis of poetry, the *sine qua non*. So then it's not, for me, *poetic* experiment, but something else, which may be all very well of its kind, but we're no longer talking about what I feel comfortable referring to as poetry. I'm aware that this puts me out on a limb, even in the 'formalist' movement, but it's that or lying to you. It is pleasure, the enormous pleasure I get from good metrical verse, and the lack of pleasure I experience when I read virtually any free verse, that has put me there.

Anyone who knows you well is aware of your loathing of Modernism. Could you expound that dislike a little?

Ah, I see that this is the part of the interview when we get Dick to fulminate. First is he opposed to poetic experiment, and then how much does he loathe Modernism? Pretty much I guess. Hard to know where to begin. I think my main feeling is that literary, poetic Modernism, to which I'll confine myself, was built on a very, very flimsy intellectual basis, and by people who were in the main charlatans, or dupes of charlatans, or worse. My real *bête noire*, as you know, is Pound. Winters has a great phrase describing him: 'a barbarian in a museum'. That's perfect, it's really what he was. All those languages he didn't know but which he quoted from and pretended to translate from. That *ex cathedra* mantle hiding basic linguistic incompetence. Ugh. Vikram Seth, who knows Chinese, says his translations from Chinese are 'compounded of ignorance of Chinese and valiant self-indulgence'. I can believe it. And since Graves's spoof, we all know what Pound's Latin was like. That's OK, of course, if you don't know Latin; fine, lots of splendid poets haven't known Latin. But for God's sake don't pretend you can translate from it. But there is something else about Pound that is for me far worse than his silly claims to learning he didn't have – it's that he was such an outrageous bully. In everything, in literature (the *ex cathedra* tone again: argument by aggressive aphorisms), in his personal relations (especially with women) and most notoriously in his politics. I know one is on tricky ground when linking politics and poetry, but I feel sure that Modernism's involvement with fascism, in the persons of Pound and Eliot, was not at all a coincidence. That sneering lumpen bullying tone which is everywhere in Pound's criticism, and which doesn't give a damn about evidence or propriety, seems wholly of a piece with a sneering lumpen bully like Mussolini, who also didn't give a damn about evidence or propriety, and whom Pound hailed as a great man. Then there was W. C. Williams, whose writings on metre are every bit as shy-making as Pound's translations. For example, he said that in his translation of the *Iliad* Chapman was attempting to reproduce in English the quantitative metre of Greek. Chapman's *Iliad* is in perfectly ordinary English accentual metre and there is nothing quantitative about it whatsoever. How can you begin to credit the remarks of someone who can make such an egregious judgement in an area (metrics) that is supposed to be of supreme importance to him, and in which he was being hailed as a guru to the young? This is all pretty *ad hominem*, I know, but I do feel that Pound was a self-promoting charlatan, that Eliot was basically a limp crypto-fascist weasel, and that Williams knew as much about meter as I know about quantum physics. How can one take seriously a movement founded and promoted by such radically shoddy minds? Another thing that really saddens me about all this is the way that free verse swept what we used to call the third world like a bacillus, so that in country after country the traditional metrical systems were infected and choked on their own blood and died. Now any number of cultures in Asia can boast their own Ezra and their own T. S. Eliot, sometimes complete with the founders' anti-Semitism too. Glory be. 'Free verse' was modernity and those countries longed for modernity, so they threw over their centuries-old literary birthrights, and for what? For very little apart from an opportunity to ruin the great work of time, as far as I can see. It makes one weep. Of course, one can see this as but an extreme example of the kind of formal syncretism we were talking about before, which in a way it is; but what makes it tragic is that there is so little cultural parity about now that there is virtually nothing to counterbalance the prestige of the West's exported literary forms. And so rather than a fusion of the indigenous and the imported one often has a virtual obliteration of the local by the extraneous. Local forms do persist, thank goodness, but often at a folk level, outside the mainstream of conscious literary endeavour. For example, in Persian-speaking countries the old poetic forms are now used largely for poems of political satire or subversion.

There are things to be said about why poetic Modernism happened (and certainly it has happened, so one has to make the best of it). From Browning on you can see that all the interesting poets were trying to do something with metre, to reinvent it in some way. The impulse is there in Swinburne and Kipling, in Morris, in Bridges's experiments with quantitative metre, in Hopkins's sprung rhythm, in Hardy's folk metres (which are often very hard to scan conventionally), in Frost's blank verse which almost becomes prose at times, so effaced is the metrical hold on the line. And then we finish up with that peculiarly repellent doctrine, very common nowadays even among people who should know better, which I think begins in Eliot's criticism, that metre is most interesting when it is violated. One might as well say that people are most interesting when they are violated. The evidence for this was mostly drawn from the verse of Shakespeare's plays, but of course that's *dramatic* verse, and Shakespeare doesn't write in this way when he is writing non-dramatic verse, the sonnets for example, or 'The Phoenix and the Turtle'. So it's irrelevant evidence. There was certainly a metrical crisis at the end of the nineteenth century in English, and I think poetry came out of it in a very bad way. The sad thing is that this, the state in which poetry emerged from that crisis, was perhaps not inevitable, and that it happened largely because of Pound, Eliot and Williams and their epigonoi. There is an alternative tradition, of course, which has never really disappeared. The crucial figure there is, I think, Auden, who though he admired Eliot took Hardy as his chief metrical model, and by his example and prestige ensured metre's survival beyond World War II. Is that wide enough an extent for my loathing?

I think that'll do, Dick. Perhaps we should change the subject. Can you comment on the role of music and visual art in what you have written?

Music has been one of the greatest sources of pleasure in my life. My family was not musical when I was a child and I wasn't encouraged to play a musical instrument. I don't think that ever occurred to anyone as an option, and besides there probably wouldn't have been the money available. But I regret that. I sometimes feel I 'should' have been a musician. I have dreamt whole operas that don't exist. What can I say? I like music very much indeed, and hardly a day goes by when I don't listen to music. I'm talking about western classical music, I'm not much good outside of that small area. I like Persian classical music too, but in a fairly unknowledgeable way. Within western music I especially like vocal music, including opera, and chamber music. I like just about any opera, but outside of opera the composers I get most pleasure from are probably Bach, Haydn, Mozart, Schubert, Stravinsky, Britten. And in something like that order of preference, which is coincidentally also their chronological order. I love line and 'argument' in music, which is maybe why I tend to prefer chamber music to orchestral music: you can hear the lines more clearly, and for an amateur like me that's important. Being a poet I love song, especially Schubert and Britten, and that isn't surprising, I guess. Purcell should be in that list too, and also Monteverdi. And I think my musical tastes have influenced my poetry. There is a kind of clear clever tender intimate wit in Haydn for example, that I'd like to be able to emulate in verse. And my care with a poem's formal construction seems somehow to do with my musical tastes. It's difficult to name specific poems, but I'm often aware of a musical ideal as I write. A little poem like 'In the Gallery' for example, seems to me to have something analogous to a musical structure. And I wrote a poem called 'A Christmas Poem' which was set by Hugh Wood, and sung at the King's College Carol Service, and then subsequently at a Carol Service in Princeton in the US. I liked it very much that the composer obviously thought the words lent themselves to music.

I tend not to like really woozy romantic music (unless it's opera, and there I'm usually happy to succumb to the emotional pornography of it all, as it were), and similarly I don't much like poetry in which everything swims together and you can't tell what the hell is going on. I don't like dark geistful chthonic stuff in any of the arts: I'm all for clarity, line and light. I'm suspicious of what can't be paraphrased. Similarly in painting, I like line and light. But there are exceptions. Rembrandt is one: some of Rembrandt makes me go weak at the knees, and I have written a few poems about him and his paintings. There it is the humane tenderness that gets me: the darkness in his paintings seems to be suffused with compassion, to be wholly without cruelty. I talked about the possibility of secular sanctity before: some of Rembrandt's works seem to inhabit or at least gesture toward that world – *The Jewish Bride*, for example, or *The Return of the Prodigal Son*, or some of his drawings and etchings of Hendrickje. That is us we feel, it *is* us and not someone angelic and impossible, but us at our human best, most tender, most giving, and so most vulnerable.

Myth – especially classical myth – has also been important for you. You have several poems that are essentially retellings of stories from Ovid or Homer. Can you account for this?

Well they are great stories, and they are emblematic for us, I suppose. I like stories in poetry – much of my scholarly work is on epic after all – and we tend not to tell stories in poems so much now, though I'm aware that some poets still do so, or have begun to do so again. Using the myths is a way of having a story in a poem. Most poets my age are conscious of Larkin's sneers at 'the myth kitty', and that has perhaps made us wary of raiding that kitty too often. But I've done it quite a bit, I guess. I think what I'm trying to do often with that kind of subject matter is to address subjects I feel uncomfortable addressing more directly. For example, in a short sequence of sonnets I wrote called 'Visitations', which are all based on myths, I talk about encounters with the numinous, something I feel almost incapable of talking about *in propria persona*. In that way, using a myth in a poem is a bit like doing a translation – it allows you to deal with a subject you feel very ambivalent about. I think it's interesting in that regard that many of my poems that use myth, and many of my translations too, deal with quasi-religious states of mind. I find religion almost impossible to write about directly in verse, and myth and translation are ways of doing so obliquely.

One thing, in connection with myth, you mention Ovid: I feel he is one of the very greatest poets of the western tradition – I mean as far as I can judge as an amateur – the equal of Virgil, say, or Dante. He's the poet in which the feminine emerges and really takes centre stage in Latin, and he's also the poet who implicitly subverts all that we find a bit uncomfortable and unpleasant about Latin culture – patriarchy and empire and all that stuff. No wonder he was exiled. And this is one matter on which I agree with Pound, his very high estimation of Golding's version of the *Metamorphoses*. He was completely right about that, and I probably wouldn't have read it if it weren't for his emphatic recommendation, so I can forgive him a lot for that and maybe I should. I suppose I might have looked at it because of Shakespeare's use of some passages, but Pound's hyperbolic praise intrigued me enough to send me in search of the whole thing (which is not that easy to find, by the way). It's a very uneven work, but it has annihilatingly beautiful things in it, some of the most poignant and delicious moments in English verse. There's a sweetness there that recalls Chaucer's *Troilus and Criseyde*, which for me is the loveliest long poem in English.

Let's move to the opposite extreme. Political realities, especially those of modern life, have always been a concern of yours. But how would you define your political position and what would you say its role was in your poetry?

I went to live in Greece and the Colonels' coup happened, I went to live in Italy and Aldo Moro was kidnapped and killed, I went to live in Iran and they had the Islamic Revolution. I began to feel like Typhoid Mary. Joking aside, I think my experiences as an adult have shown me how very fragile relatively open societies are, and how easily they can be destroyed. They have also given me a real fear of the mob, revolutionary or whatever it might call itself: when mobs pull people from their houses and kill them in the street they are simply mobs, and ideology is neither here nor there. As a young man from a relatively underprivileged background I was your typical undergraduate socialist, and I still have some sympathy for that position. I still instinctively doubt the words and intentions of those with power and privilege, and I feel with Graham Greene that 'of course one always sides with the victim, that goes without saying'. Identifying the victim, though, is another matter. Who, for example, is the victim in the middle east? Just about everybody is the honest answer. As you get older you see complexity, and complexity can be paralyzing for decision and action. My chief political concern now is that openness be preserved, that fanaticisms be blunted and rendered harmless, that the lines be kept open between factions who are ready to loathe one another. It is crystal clear, I feel, that utopian totalizing solutions ('If only there were true socialism / true Islam / true Christianity … If only there were no Moslems / no Jews / no Americans …') *ipso facto* lead to bloodshed, bloodshed which never, ever brings the promised utopia, and so is simply pointless. So, like many as they get older, I am suspicious of utopian schemes, and

I am all for gradual piecemeal amelioration where it is possible. I have become cautious and middle-aged, and I have a deep fear of political violence, having seen it, had friends killed by it, and seen other friends broken by the torture meted out in revolutionary prisons. I have not yet reached the stage that Goethe got to when he said 'Better injustice than anarchy', and I sincerely hope I never do get to that stage, but I begin to imagine the state of mind in which one might be afraid enough to say that. I am very, very pessimistic about the political state of the world. But then I reflect on how the world looked in 1939, and that the world pulled through, largely because my parents' generation didn't panic and fall to pieces. So, neither must we. My poetry rarely addresses politics directly, though it is often concerned with individuals who get caught up in political processes that redirect and sometimes ruin their lives. Most of my books have at least one or two poems in which that is the basic subject matter. There's 'Fraulein X' from *The Covenant* for example, 'On the Iranian Diaspora' and 'Mohsen' from *A Kind of Love*, 'Middle East 1950s' from *Lares*, 'To 'Eshqi', from *Touchwood*, 'Political Asylum' from *Belonging*, and so on. I'm not at all, though, a political poet, and my poems deal with individuals, not causes, classes, nations or religions. But I hope I am a compassionate poet. Of course I am wholly aware that compassion is very lenten fare for the victims of misused political power.

About half-way through your career, you became a rather unusual love poet, it seems to me. This might be thought surprising: one expects the younger poet to be strong on love, but your concern has perhaps increased with age. Would it be even true to say that in your later work love occupies the place of history in the early poems?

Maybe. Yes, I think I'd accept that. It's partly to do with realizing that one has only one life to live, so one might as well get on and live it. I've been, I guess, lucky in love: but that seems a very risky thing to say and also I don't want to get into mawkish personal detail. In a way many of my poems that perhaps to others don't seem like love poems are love poems for me: almost all my poems on Iran and Persian culture, for example, are also overt or covert love poems. I guess another reason I write about love is to do with my lack of a secure religion coupled with an interest in many of the things that a religion often caters to. Those emotions that might have found a home in religion spill over into love poems to people. It's not love in the sense of erotic desire, though I'm all for that too, so much as in the sense of gratitude and wonder. That kind of thing. And it's to do with something I mentioned before, the sense that one should encourage and grasp possibilities of happiness wherever one finds them. Love, especially when one is young, can mean great unhappiness of course, but the other possibility is there too. I wish I could express my love for my children more often and more clearly in poems: I still find that hard for some reason, perhaps because children are so protean and so one isn't sure the whole time what it is one is loving, though I have written some poems to and for them. I feel a superstitious sense of hubris in saying all this, so can we pass on to something else?

OK! Complete change of tack! You have become a distinguished translator of Persian poetry. (You have done both Attar and Ferdowsi, for instance). Do you regard that as part of your own work as a poet?

Yes and no. I enjoy making verse translations very much: there is something extraordinarily satisfying about taking a poem in one language and turning it into what you hope is a roughly equivalent poem in another language. The attempt to bring off the trick of capturing both fidelity and beauty in a verse version of someone else's work is the keenest intellectual pleasure I know of, probably because it combines both a measure of creativity and a measure of scholarship at one and the same time. But certainly it's not the same as writing one's own poems. One thing that is perhaps relevant is that it's very hard to judge in any objective way one's own poems – sometimes they seem dreadful and sometimes they seem wonderful, and one never really knows what they are. But one can be more objective about a verse translation; you can tell yourself you're doing something useful. It's good that poems that haven't had any embodiment at all in English now have one, even if someone else in ten or fifteen or a hundred years might make a much better version. So you're relieved of the nagging worry that it's all a waste of time, which I think afflicts most poets at least occasionally when they are writing their own poems. I've learnt a lot technically from making verse translations: you have to have a good repertoire of technical tricks if you're to produce a lot of verse translations. Basic things like instinctively ending lines with words you're likely to be able to find rhymes for, and not ending them with words that have virtually no rhymes; the ability to lay the syntax of a narrative across successive lines, which is quite tricky until you get the knack of it; an awareness of when to leaven a long poem with the surface interest of things like alliteration or grammatical parallelism between lines. Those kinds of thing, all of which are learnable. This mechanical apprenticeship has been very useful to me in writing some of my own poems, especially the longer ones.

The actual process of verse translation I find really fascinating; the way, for example, that it is something self-consciously cerebral, in which you have to have your wits about you and you want your mind to be functioning as clearly and sharply as possible, and then how at the same time you have to hope for the serendipitous, the peculiar whatever it is that throws up the right phrase in the right context from the mind's depths. Both these levels are there in writing one's own poems, of course, but I think they are much more obviously there when doing a verse translation. Apart from knowledge of the languages involved, and a kind of linguistic tact and respect for what is there, the ability to have your mind switch constantly between these two levels is I think the most important quality a good verse translator needs. And of course you have to be both a good reader and a good writer, and you have to be both almost in the same moment. That too is relatively rare as a combination, I think.

I'm drawn to verse translation too because it's hard, often very hard if it's done at all competently, 'the fascination of what's difficult' as Yeats said. And also – and I guess this is a bit curmudgeonly of me – because it's despised, both by scholars because it isn't a literal crib, and by poets because it isn't obviously original work, as you're submitting your sensibility, to the extent that you can, to someone else's. There are incoming shells from both sides, as it were. I'm pretty sure that another reason I like verse translation so much is that it is almost impossible not to fail at it. This is almost comforting in a way, as it frees you from the burden of insisting to yourself that you succeed. Of course you do your best, and you are very conscious of being admonished by the author you are translating to do your best (or at least I am), especially if he or she is dead, as most authors I've translated are. But, as I say, you're certain to fail, as all verse translations are necessarily approximations and necessarily partial approximations at that. If one is allowed to have favourites among one's own poems, one of my poems that I feel most affection for is called 'A Translator's Nightmare', in which I go through – in what I hope is a humorous way – the possibilities of failure that await a verse translator.

Are there other poets you ever think of translating – Hafez for instance, or Rumi?

They are both very difficult poets to translate. The history of Persian scholarship in English is littered with failed attempts to produce a readable Hafez. Hafez is a very allusive and elusive poet, and one who exploits the conventions of medieval Persian poetry, which are wholly different from the conventions of English poetry, to the utmost. I have in fact been asked to do a Hafez by a publisher, but I don't think I can. I have done one or two of his poems, but they don't really work that well in my versions. Or in anyone else's, come to that. I might try again: but believe me, it's very hard. I'm trying to think of an analogy in English. Imagine trying to translate 'The Wreck of the Deutschland' into Arabic. Something of that nature. Rumi is different: Rumi is a great poet, no question of that, but he's not really my kind of a great poet. You know the hedgehog / fox distinction Isaiah Berlin made between kinds of writers? Well, Rumi is a real fox, lots and lots of tricks, quite unpindownable. A real shape-shifter. You need someone with a big Tolstoyan grasp to translate Rumi. The verse translations of his poetry that are current in the west are in general abysmally bad, and give almost no sense of what he's like in Persian. To begin with, he's a very learned poet: you'd never guess that from the New Age versions of Rumi that clog the bookstores nowadays. Really the only writer you can compare him to in English is Shakespeare: he's protean and endlessly inventive, and magically unpredictable, in a Shakespearian kind of way. He's beyond my grasp to do well, I feel, and I don't want to do him badly. No point in that. And as I say, I don't feel he's my poet, I don't feel inward with him as I do with Attar, for example. You know that Wentworth Dillon in his *Essay on Verse Translation* says to the prospective translator, 'Choose an author as you choose a friend': I don't really feel that Rumi and I are cut out to be friends. Maybe later I'll change my mind, but I think it's more likely I'll try Hafez than Rumi. And if I'm sensible I'll probably try neither. There are some other poets I'd like to translate. There is a wonderful woman poet who was a contemporary of Hafez, so she was fourteenth century, and she lived in the same city as he did, Shiraz. Her name was Jahan Khatun, and I would like to do a substantial number of her poems, perhaps as a little book. I've done a few already. She's a really super poet – witty, passionate and very feisty. A bit like Louise Labé or Gaspara Stampa, but with a charming, flirtatious side that is not so obvious in their work.

In recent years there have been some longer poems. I think especially of 'Esther' in Touchwood. *Is writing such poems something you feel you ought to do to extend your range, or are they just as exigent as the short poems? Are they volitional or written out of need?*

'Esther' was written as a commission. It's a rather unfortunate story. A fine press publisher wanted me to do something chapbook length that was a narrative, that was Persian, and that was Jewish. Well, that considerably restricts one's options, and Esther seemed the obvious and maybe only choice. So I duly wrote the poem, and then he went bankrupt and closed down his press and went into the insurance business. 'Esther' was left on my hands so I put her in what was then my next book, *Touchwood*, to fill it out. I'm not sure she really belongs there. The model for 'Esther' was Auden's long sequential poems, like *The Age of Anxiety* and *The Sea and the Mirror*, especially the latter. Mention of Auden reminds me of something: he once said that he went around with forms in his head and subjects in his head, and when they came together he had a poem. That has happened to me with long poems. For example, 'A Letter to Omar', a longish poem in my third book, *The Covenant*, was written largely because I wanted to do something in the Kháyyám stanza form, and Afkham's and my flight from Iran provided me with a subject. And in *Belonging*, the longest poem is 'Teresia Sherley'. This historical character is someone I've wanted to write a poem on for many years, nearly twenty years, in fact. And for five years or so I'd wanted to write a reasonably long poem in the form that Browning used for 'A Toccata of Galuppi's', which is easily my favourite Browning poem. And then one day those two separate wishes coalesced and I was able to start the poem. That's a love poem, by the way, to return to a previous question, a really all-out love poem. As to whether such poems are volitional or written out of need, I guess all long poems have to be volitional to some extent, simply because you can't complete even a first draft in one sitting, so there has to be volition to carry you over to when you try again, and extend the poem.

I've known and loved your poetry for forty years, so perhaps I can be allowed to lodge a faint objection to some of it. It seems to me that you have a weakness for resolving problems and for tying things up in your poems a little too neatly. Do you feel any anxiety on this score yourself, and can you defend your work against this reservation of mine?

I guess it's the epigrammatic-closure instinct we talked about before, that in some poems strikes you as an inappropriate way to resolve things. What can I say? I like clarity and try for it, I don't like to leave things unresolved. It's temperamental, as we said before. Mystery, real mystery, I feel is sacred, but so much of modern poetry deals in factitious mystery. I don't want factitious mystery – hocus-pocus – in my poems, and perhaps I push too hard to excise it. I'd rather, all things being equal, err on the side of neatness than of mess, and what a prissy old maid that makes me sound. But it's so. No, I can't defend myself against your stricture, and you are not the only person to have said it, or something like it, by any means. I don't think I will change my practice, though. I don't think I could. It would be like forcing someone who's left-handed to be right-handed, and I'm too old for that now.

Conversely, the poems I like best are those which leave me with a sense of something unresolved, a sense of the irreducible mystery of simply being in the world. To name some examples: 'What the Mind Wants', 'Desert Stop at Noon', 'Night on the Long-Distance Coach', 'Iran Twenty Years Ago' – these are just named at random. Do you yield readily to this feeling or does it frustrate the rationalist in your make up?

I feel that real poetry is written out of mysteries that we try to understand. I hate it when poets manufacture mystery instead of trying to understand the mystery that is there, when they import it into their poems, smear it on them from outside. Ersatz surrealism, telling a story and missing out crucial details, introducing privacies no one outside your circle can recognize, flouting grammar – the whole dreary gamut of Modernist mystification. This all seems to me to be fake poetry, pretend poetry, not real poetry. The reader – or this reader anyway – feels conned, led up the garden path. I don't want to con the reader, or to con myself. Poetry for me records the attempt to understand; the last thing it wants to do is obfuscate. But sometimes there are things we can't understand: we go as far as we can and then if we're honest we stop. Poems of mine that are like that are, to use a distinction you just offered, really written out of need rather than volition. I would like to understand, that's what I really want to do, but I recognize that I can't. So I stop. I like those poems too, but you're right that they do frustrate the rationalist in me. I think poets should be rationalists for as far as they possibly can be. That they should give it up only as a very last resort. But sometimes you have to, if you're to stay honest.

Rachel Hadas

photo courtesy of
Roy Groething

A NOTE ON RACHEL HADAS

Rachel Hadas was born in 1948 and spent her childhood in New York City. She studied classics at Harvard, poetry at Johns Hopkins University, and comparative literature at Princeton. During the early Seventies, between college and graduate school, she spent four years in Greece. There she met and became friends with James Merrill. Since 1981 she has taught in the English Department at the Newark, New Jersey, campus of Rutgers University. She has also taught occasional courses in literature and writing at Princeton and Columbia and has occasionally served on the poetry faculty of the Sewanee Writers' Conference. She has published twelve books of verse, essays and translations and has received several awards, including a Guggenheim Fellowship in Poetry, two Ingram Merrill Foundation grants in poetry and an award in literature from the American Academy and Institute of Arts and Letters. Her collection, *Halfway down the Hall: New and Selected Poems,* published by Wesleyan in 1998, was a finalist for the 1999 Lenore Marshall Poetry Prize.

With her home background – her father was the renowned classicist Moses Hadas – and her education in the classics, the Greek experience figures frequently in Hadas's early verse, particularly in *Slow Transparency* of 1983, and it surfaces again in some later poems. Unsurprisingly, both George Seferis's work – with its vision of sea and islands, the residues of time, classical myth and history – and James Merrill's – with its wordplay, citation, cutting and intercutting – had early impacts on her writing.

Her later poetry, however, has become much more independent. The language games are subordinated by an awareness of more contemporary things, the more local limits of living. In *Pass It On* (1989), themes of friendship, marriage, and the relations between parent and child are foregrounded. Poems deal unsentimentally with domestic themes such as child-bearing and nursing, reading children stories, watching them learning to master speech and language. *Indelible* (2001), while touching on themes from her earlier work, traces the contours and the erosions of time in the terrain of family, art, and literature, elegy and dream. The book also contains some prose poems, perhaps an innovation, though her prose and poems have always run closely parallel. As Rosanna Warren remarked: 'Her traffic with the ordinary – closet-cleaning, recycling paper, sorting files – goes on under the gaze of the ancient gods.'

In 2000, she published a book of essays and reminiscences, *Merrill, Cavafy, Poems, and Dream,* in the Poets on Poetry Series of the University of Michigan Press. Here her Greek reminiscences, and memories of James Merrill and Alan Ansen provide background to the poems. There is also a spirited defence, as one might expect from a classicist, of the formal aspects of poetry, though Hadas has never been too regimental about this in the way that some of the New Formalists are. In using the ballade form in 'The End of Summer', a poem to her son, she remarks: 'should this rigid rhyme / scheme leave you cramped ...' – A New Formalist might well think her use of the form here licentious in its use of oblique rhymes.

A note on Isaac Cates

Isaac Cates is Assistant Professor of English and Director of the Poetry Center at the C. W. Post campus of Long Island University. He was born in 1971 in Germany, and spent most of his youth on a small ranch south of Austin, Texas. He holds degrees from the University of Texas at Austin, Johns Hopkins University, and Yale University. He has published poems in *Southwest Review* and *Cumberland Poetry Review,* and essays on contemporary poetry in *Literary Imagination* and in several handbooks and encyclopedias. With Mike Wenthe he has also written and drawn a series of comic books and short pieces that have appeared in *Other* and *Backwards City Review*. Since the summer of 1998 he has written more than fourteen thousand postcards. He is currently writing a book on the graphic novel for Yale University Press. He lives in New Haven, Connecticut.

Rachel Hadas in conversation with Isaac Cates

It seems the best way to begin would be chronologically, where the narrative or your poetic career seems to begin, with your move from America to Greece in the early '70s.

I graduated from college in '69 and went to Greece on a very Henry-Jamesian little fellowship called the Isobel M. Briggs Travelling Fellowship, which was all of a thousand dollars. I didn't really move to Greece; I meant to be travelling here and there, but I felt really at home in Athens. Also in many ways I didn't know what else to do with myself.

You could equally have said my life as a poet began when my father died, which was after my first year in college. But I think the fact that I then stuck around in Greece after a brief move back to America, then lived in Greece again for four years – this, with getting to know James Merrill there, not studying any more, and just sort of living, learning a language: it was enormously, enormously important.

In retrospect, however, it doesn't feel like a move to Greece: it just feels like a very few years spent there, in a life that's getting longer and longer.

Although I imagine that, at the time, there must have been some illusion of permanence.

For a little while.

I'm wondering: your father, Moses Hadas, was a well-known (even famous) classicist, and, as you said, he died when you were just starting college. To what extent was travelling to Greece and lingering there related to your father's scholarly interests?

When I was growing up, we never travelled abroad; my father thought the best way to get work done was to stay home. So in going to Greece I was treating myself to an adventure, seeing places I'd only read about – but of course, yes, also in some way, going in search of a father who was not only a classicist but who had been in the O.S.S., had spent time in Athens (as well as in Cairo and Cyprus), and had Greek friends, some of whom I met when I was first in Athens. This was never a well-defined mission, but it was always somewhere in the cloudy or over-determined mix of a young person's motives.

I'm curious, too, about your friendship with James Merrill. Had you known him, or known his work, before you met him in Athens? How did you meet? Merrill was fairly established as a poet by the early '70s.

John Hollander, who was a family friend (and who had accepted my poem 'Daddy' for *Harper's* while I was an undergraduate at Harvard) said, 'If you're going to be in Athens, you absolutely must look up Jimmy Merrill,' which I did, and I fell in love with Merrill instantly – fell in love with everything about him. It was as if I'd always known him. We took to each other at once. But everyone always took to Merrill.

That's certainly his reputation. Was it through Merrill that you met Alan Ansen? Ansen is not as well known, but I take it he was also a sort of early mentor to you.

Alan Ansen was a great friend and teacher from the time I met him in the fall of 1969 onwards. I've written about him (in 'Fructifying a Cycle', which is in *Merrill, Cavafy, Poems, and Dreams*) and learned from him steadily, and our lives have been intertwined in numerous ways. In fact, I'm his literary executor, and I hope to visit him in Athens in a few weeks.

What were the circumstances of your meeting? In a way you seem a very unlikely pair: his 'raucous yawp', as you have it in that essay, which he seems to owe to Ginsberg, sounds very far from your poetic voice. (I'm thinking of his line about the 'ululant leap in skivvies through snickering respectable streets', which you quote in that essay). It's a little hard to imagine being the person to make introductions between the two of you.

I seem to remember Alan Ansen's name was, like Merrill's, given to me by John Hollander. Anyway it was inevitable that I met Alan once I started circulating in the little pond of American writers in Athens. Bernie Winebaum, an occasional poet and aesthete, for example, lived across the hall from Alan.
    Alan was alarming, energizing, welcoming, mysterious, hospitable, utterly unique. Maybe he represented something I needed – which was mutual. I also understood and enjoyed the incongruity of our friendship from the start.

Was poetry the text, or the subtext – or really only a pretext – for these friendships with Merrill and Ansen? That is, were you mainly friends who happened to be poets, or were you seeing and influencing each other's poems? Were they keen to help you 'become' a poet?

Merrill's and Ansen's being poets certainly played a role in our friendships, but they never nudged me to be or become a poet, and they never showed me their drafts. I would have been too shy to ask. They were adults who were writers whom I encountered as friends (or who became friends), not as teachers. I hope this isn't either too obscure or too obvious!

No, that's a good answer. I'm just trying to probe a little into the way your time in Greece shaped your decision – if there was a conscious one – to become a professional poet or professional writer.
   I guess the reason I'm locating this decision in Greece has to do with your poem 'A Copy of Ariel', and with the essay 'Word by Word, Page by Page', where you talk about the project of translating the Plath poem, 'Poppies in July', into Greek. That seems like the moment when, even though you say that it was a sort of effort against yourself, in a way –

' ... making one more effort to efface / the person I had always been.'

That's it. You don't describe it as a moment of coming into your own, but does that moment stand out as one in which you imagined your poetic or literary life as being more public, or professional? Was this a moment when you started to imagine publishing? What were the circumstances behind the publication of Starting from Troy?

It was kind of the opposite of coming into my own. In 'Mornings in Ormos', I say that people complimented me on my Greek by saying, 'Have you forgotten English?' (God forbid.) So, translating 'Poppies in July' may have been an attempt to enact being Greek, but it turned out that it wasn't really do-able.
   The publication of my first book, *Starting from Troy*, in 1975, followed my return from Greece in 1974. I don't recall that there was a causal nexus. I do remember that James Merrill very kindly read the proofs of *Starting from Troy*, which was pretty exciting, in Athens – it would have been in the spring of 1974.
   How long ago and remote all that seems. In one way, Greece was absolutely crucial for my work and the course of my career, but, in another

way, it was an aberration, because I was living in an unbookish society while I was on Samos, and that made me incredibly lonely. The rest of my life on both sides of that interlude has been absolutely lined with books, and in many ways much more comfortable.

That phrase, 'lined with books', immediately puts me in mind of the title poem in Halfway down the Hall, *where you depict the space in which you're reading as a sort of niche between bookshelves that extend down the hall on either side of you. Certainly your homes here in America have always held plenty of bookshelves.*

In my parents' apartment at 460 Riverside, I faced a wall of books when I sat at the dining room table. After my father died, some of these books were sold, and the gaps were very upsetting to me. Children are very conservative; any change is terrible. It was an enactment of loss, in a way.

Native to this scholarly environment as you are, your work – though it doesn't plume itself on allusion or bookishness – has a strong sense of a literary and literate context. The way you describe living in Ormos, on the other hand, it seems that the number of books that you had at hand was finite and countable: you could run down a list of the books you had in English.

Absolutely – which is also a valuable experience. You come to depend on memory. You come to realize, like Erich Auerbach, who went to Istanbul to escape the Nazis – instead of going West he went East – that to some extent you have your library in your head. I've written about that recently in an essay on poetry anthologies. What is a poetry anthology? Empson, I think, in China, said it's what you have in your head.

As long as we're thinking about the finite number of books you had in Ormos, could you list the ones you remember?

I'm sure there were more than I remember, but all right: there was my Faber and Faber British paperback edition, ordered from Blackwell's, of Sylvia Plath's *Ariel*, which I still have. I've described the way that book smells.

You would have to keep it, after having written so memorably about that particular copy.

And about the mouse-nibblings in it, and so forth. I had one of those Norton or Houghton Mifflin Riverside copies of Wordsworth. I had some Jane Austen. My sister very kindly sent me two omnibus books: one of them was the complete novels of Dashiell Hammett, which was great, and one was an omnibus of five selected novels by Ross MacDonald, who is a wonderful mystery writer in the school of Raymond Chandler. I prefer him to Chandler. I just memorized them.

John Irwin talks about keeping a copy of Maltese Falcon *handy and reading it about twice a year. As you know, he's been working on these long poems,* Just Let Me Just Say This About That *and* As Long as It's Big, *which he wants to have a very American idiom, and in order to re-attune his ear to that, he regularly re-reads* Maltese Falcon.

I should have tried to translate Hammett into Greek.

I remember, now I come to think of it, one of the American tourists who floated through Samos was an old professor from Florida, with whom I discussed an idea I had for writing an essay comparing Mrs Norris in *Mansfield Park* to the meddling aunt in *Washington Square*. So I was pretty literary. I can't remember if I had the Henry James in front of me; presumably I did. I had *Middlemarch*, too. And then whatever Alan Ansen would lend me when I'd go to Athens. Or obviously I could buy books there. Still, my bookshelf was pretty skimpy.

I suppose you would not have imagined at that point that you'd be in graduate school, surrounded with books again, a few years later.

I think I was trying not to imagine a future. But eventually it became impossible not to realize that the present wasn't working. My mother on one visit brought me a copy of Germaine Greer's *The Female Eunuch*. That was an interesting move on her part.

I also remember having Betty Friedan's *The Feminine Mystique* with me. My mother brought me also Erica Jong's *Fear of Flying*, which was new at that time (in the 1970s) and which actually mentioned my father, in the section where Jong talks about going out with Columbia undergraduates while she was at Barnard. My mother may have liked the book chiefly because it mentioned my father, but I liked it for other reasons.

What did I imagine about the future? I don't know. I don't know what I imagined. It's a good question.

Were you composing the poems that would be in Starting from Troy *at that time, or were they mostly composed after you returned to the States?*

I'd have to look and see if I could remember, but one or two of the poems in *Starting from Troy*, I blush to say, were written while I was still in high school: 'The Fall of Troy', which begins, 'Sing now the heavy furniture of the fall ...'

That's quite a triumph for a high-school poem.

Even at the time, I think I knew this was the first real poem I'd ever written. And the poem called 'Daddy', about my father's death – the first of many – I wrote while I was in college.

You write about that poem having been written before the supposed moratorium on writing about your father's death had elapsed. 'Stay off it six weeks, one said. / No. Only pulling at the past / can bring me up to what is dead.'

That's right. Some of the poems in that book I did write in Athens, and some in Samos, and some of them were written when I was back in America, but very much thinking about Greece. One of your preliminary questions had to do with my two places of residence now, in New York and Vermont, and where did I do my writing, and I think it gets all mushed up. I by no means only wrote about Greece while I was in Greece.

In fact, there's a poem about your time in Ormos in Indelible. *The title of 'Samian Morning, 1971' announces the fact that, in a book published in 2001, it's looking back thirty years. And yet the landscape – the material – as it returns in your work, still seems fresh.*

And in fact 'Samian Morning, 1971' is quite recent: it would have been written some time in the 1990s. And why? Why did I write that poem then? Or another way of putting it would be, why couldn't I have written a poem like that when I was twenty-five? But I don't think I could have.

Well, I think one of the things about 'Samian Morning, 1971' that marks it as a poem belonging in Indelible *is the concern with physical objects passing from one person to another – I suppose it's a theme that runs through a lot of your poems, but this cashmere sweater you say you give to the gypsy woman, and which she rejects because it has this stain –*

And you know what? The stain's indelible. Incredibly, I think I just figured that out.

Sure. I've underlined it: 'A stain like a port wine birthmark'.

People who don't understand poetry are always surprised at the intuitive way some poets work. I did not plan that indelible stain. As far as the objects being passed on, I have a book called *Pass It On*. But you were saying?

I was also thinking of the poem 'Recycling', where you take over ownership of these manila folders in which Charles Barber kept files on his favourite writers, and where the folders are chiefly handled as physical objects – paper to be reused or recycled. Or 'My Mother's Closet', in which you literally 'rummage through / the wardrobes of the dead'. You had alluded earlier to the meaning picked up by your specific copy of Ariel *or by the individual books your father had owned: these books are physical objects, not only the literature they contain. This is something I see running through a lot of your work – not only articulated in* Indelible, *certainly, but very important there.*

It's almost like something that Elaine Scarry ascribes to the world of Thomas Hardy in Resisting Representation. *Hardy is so interested in tangible things in the world, and their having been used already when they come into someone else's hands, that a used violin bears on it the sheen of having been played by someone else years ago. Or the walls have a stain where a house's inhabitants place their hands on a doorjamb when passing by. It's something about the physical evidence of use.*

That's interesting about Hardy. One poem of mine that illustrates what you're talking about is 'Rag Rug'. The rug in that poem is a combination of a cloth household object and also something that's recycled, because the Samian women used looms – amazing Homeric looms – to weave these rugs. I used to spend time ripping things like old nightgowns into strips and sewing the strips together and rolling balls of rags. It was a great pleasure to me that these balls could be transformed into beautiful rugs.

And I have a poem in *A Son From Sleep* called 'Little by Little', which has the line, 'And there are other signs of tender wear. / Cats softly rub their chins on edges they make dingy.'

That's nice. That's very much like Hardy. And the poem 'Rag Rug', I think, which begins Halfway down the Hall, *does a nice job of combining the two images that are repeated here in* Indelible: *the sweater that becomes a rag, and the paper cut into tiny strips to be re-used as bookmarks in 'Recycling'. 'Recycling' is, I suppose, on a theme that seems at first very trivial – a description of household habits – but it opens up in a really interesting way to be about the physical embodiment of ideas, and how the physical thing remains around.*

In a way, that physical thing is transformed, and, in a way, it's simply shrunken or distilled. Merrill puts it so beautifully in his memoirs, where he asks, 'Wouldn't I too turn, word by word, page by page, into books on a shelf?' The occasion is his return from his trip to Europe, when he's in his twenties; his friend the Dutch poet Hans Lodeizen had recently died of leukemia. Hans's first and last book of poems arrives in New York, and it's as if Merrill has the essence, or what remains, of Hans between covers. Of course I quote that passage in 'Word by Word, Page by Page'.
    Over the years, I think my poems have become a lot more accessible to people. Although I'm not particularly a poet of things of this world – I don't think I'm a great observer – I do think that perhaps in *Indelible* there are more tangible, visualizable objects than in my earlier poems. People take great pleasure in recognizing things they know.
    It can't be a coincidence that 'The Red Hat' is my single most popular poem. It speaks to issues of parenthood, yes, but then there's that vivid little cloth object in it.

It's a poem that you can see the picture in.

And that seems to be really important. To say another word about that question of 'Do I write poems about images that can be visualized?': when I look back at the early poems written in Greece, many of which are in *Slow Transparency*, not just *Starting From Troy*, I often think the fault of those poems is that they're too lush, too adjectival, and too much attempting to capture the beauty of a landscape I would have done better to take pictures of, or to paint.
    I say to my students, 'Poems are not for making pictures. That's not all they're for.' That's not enough, for poems. It's not enough, and it's too much, at the same time.

Right. Well, because pictures do the job better.

Pictures often do the job much better.

There's something along those lines in 'Samian Morning, 1971', where you say, 'Had I looked ... beyond her, / I would have seen the Aegean like a frame. / If I had looked far enough over her right shoulder, / I would have seen Patmos ...' and then, 'Over her left / shoulder I could have craned and seen Ionia.' And there's this sense that there's a potential for making a sort of landscape description there, and instead you focus on the human relationship between the figures in the poem.
    Although, now that I look at it: the beginning of the next stanza lays out a series of landmarks, a schematic topography: 'Where had she come from?' Well, 'behind the house was a field. / Beyond this ... / were a bent fig tree and a low stone wall / and a whitewashed hut.' But that's a landscape remembered and not seen.

It's reconstructed, it's put back together.

I mean, you're not making an effort there to describe a picture so much as to draw a kind of map: the sort of map you draw for someone to accompany verbal directions. You don't spend adjectives on the fig tree –

Although I could, and probably did, more, in earlier poems. One reason my earlier poems are often embarrassing to me is that either they're too adjectival, too much trying to make pictures, as I said, or else they're too abstract. One extreme or the other: they don't seem to be able to focus on a subject. And they're too talky. I see lots of problems in them.

I'd like to try out an analogy to painting: in a museum, people, the patrons, walk by still-lifes pretty quickly. Or landscapes. Merely descriptive painting doesn't hold your attention in the same way as something that's painted with equal skill and composed equally well, but has a human figure in it. People are more interested if you put a person in there.

I always say to my students: even if it purports to be about Pogo Possum or some sci-fi robot, literature is by people, it's for people, and it's about people.

Well, Pogo is probably more human than many of the people we know.

To go back to painting: I've seen one or two comparisons of Marilyn Hacker's work to Dutch painting. Nothing could be more misleading. It's true that Marilyn Hacker's capable of writing 'I went to the *boulangerie* and I bought a baguette, and I had a baguette with honey, and the sun came in the window.' She does like to create interiors. But there's an uneasy spirit, a historical consciousness, love problems, and a lot of other human ambivalences at work in her poems.

And they're much more narrative than a painting could ever be. Even a genre painting can't hold as much narrative as even a relatively lyric poem conveys quite easily.

Speaking of narrative in paintings, I have two *ecphrastic* (as they like to say now) poems in *The Empty Bed*: 'Four Lives, Stirring' and 'The Red House'. The latter poem is addressing a painting by Malevich, of that name, a painting that at one point I wanted to have on the cover of the book, though that wasn't to be. 'Four Lives, Stirring' is based on one of my workshops at Gay Men's Health Crisis where we had postcards on the table. People unsurprisingly did their best to make a narrative out of these four images. And then if they know, reading it, that it's postcards, they'll try to identify who the painter is. All kinds of interesting things happen.
    We've moved far from Greece, haven't we?

We have. After your return to the States in 1974, then, what motivated your decision to do graduate work, first at Hopkins and then at Princeton?

Finding myself back in America, ending my first (or Greek, or starter) marriage, realizing poetry was what I felt most passionate about, being curious about going back to school – college – all these elements converged when I discovered a one-year MA programme on the East Coast that even offered teaching fellowships. One year wasn't too daunting a commitment. It wasn't until I found myself back on campus that I realized I loved being a student again – and a teacher.
    Meanwhile, it soon became obvious that, in the immortal words of George Edwards (the composer I met at the MacDowell Colony the summer before I went to Hopkins – we were married two years later), 'An MA and a token will get you a ride on the subway.' Being back in school had felt right; going for a PhD was the obvious next move. Why Princeton? I wanted to hold onto my Modern Greek, and Edmund Keeley was at Princeton. Comparative Literature enabled me both to eat and to keep my classical cake; and I wanted to be near New York.

What were the two programmes like, comparatively, for you? Undertaking a PhD doesn't seem to have decided you in favour of literary criticism – in fact, you've written that in the introduction to your dissertation you said, 'I am a poet first and any other kind of writer second' – but did you prefer the literature classroom to the workshop model?

I don't think I've ever been very good at workshopping my poems. The only poetry workshop I took as an undergraduate, for instance, was from Robert Fitzgerald, at Harvard. I steered clear of Lowell, who scared me. And Lowell's acolytes scared me. Fitzgerald was a very gentle taskmaster.

A lot of people who worked with Fitzgerald as undergraduates are now poets well-known for a certain facility with form, if not as New Formalists.

Lots. There was even a group photograph of us at one time. In 1988, there was a reading at Yale – it was not long after Fitzgerald's death, and I think Penny Laurans organized it. People who had studied with Robert came and gave a memorial reading. There were – off the top of my head – Judith Baumel, Dana Gioia, Mary Jo Salter, Jacqueline Osherow, myself, Robert Shaw, Brad Leithauser ... and I'm drawing a blank, but I'm sure there were sundry others.

It's an impressive group, certainly. There was something I had wanted to ask, in the manner of that clueless interviewer in A Hard Day's Night *who asks Ringo 'Are you a mod, or a rocker?' (you know, he answers: 'I'm a mocker.'), but with a little more seriousness: are you a poet, or a critic?*
By which, all I really mean is this: in all three of your books with essays – The Double Legacy, Living in Time, *and* Unending Dialogue *– the relationship between poetry and prose, even in books that are predominantly prose, is very organic. The themes that you're looking at in some of the essays come back in the poems and vice-versa.*

I think 'organic' is very polite. There are other ways we could describe it, such as porous: anything can get through.
  For somebody who feels as strongly as I do about literature, and good writing, I confess that my sense of my own poetry and prose is probably somewhat peculiar. It seems to be intuitive to the point of inscrutability. You know, 'Why is this a poem, why is this prose?' Not to say that my

poems are prosy: they're not, if only because they're in metre. But I have been known to draft poems that turn out to be sort of lazy essays. I look back at them and I think, 'I'm working out an idea here, but I'm doing it in a very telegraphic way,' and when I've unpacked my ideas more, it turns out to be something more like prose. And then sometimes it goes the other way.

For example, my essay 'Classics' began as a poem that was sort of semi-commissioned by *Arion*. The poetic process freed me up to remember lots of details, such as how the doorman at 460 Riverside used to sneeze. The actual poem, however, was really quite boring. It was ten pages, and rather loose and prosaic. I thought about it, and I thought both 'I have more to say' and 'This doesn't hold the reader's interest.'

Part of my process reminds me of a bird building a nest: the bird thinks, 'Oh, darn; better go get some more straws and insert them somehow.'

That's actually a metaphor that Louise Glück uses in a poem in Vita Nova. *Or if not a metaphor, a parable: she has a poem called 'Nest' in which a bird gathers up the remnants of things in the yard after everything has died in the winter. Gradually it is able to form a nest. There's a line I really like: she says, 'But when was there suddenly* mass?' *These brittle twigs have been laid against each other, and soon the mass of the structure itself is holding the structure together.*

Talk about recycling.

I can imagine a nest, actually, built of the twig-like scraps of paper you describe in 'Recycling'. I keep coming back to that image because it's familiar to me from around my house: miscellaneous little scraps of paper used as bookmarks.

My father, who smoked a lot, would take a matchbook, open it, and then cut the cardboard into tiny little bookmarks: recycling. And then also, my mother grew up during the Depression, as I say in the poem 'Recycling'; at Bryn Mawr the girls made their skirts out of drapery, very much like Scarlett O'Hara.

As I get older, my own attitude toward clothing and adornment is, 'If I can keep my mind and my body in reasonably good shape, that's the main thing.' We're deceived into wanting to acquire new things, but who needs new things? The trick is to stay alive.

I have a copy of The Moonstone *that I picked up second-hand in Baltimore: a cheap paperback. It had something like fifteen pieces of paper in it: receipts, a boarding pass, a business card for somebody in Sweden (named, I'm not making this up, 'Jessica Scheme'). All the receipts were in pounds, from shops in Dorking. My roommate and I deduced a sort of narrative, and a plan to blackmail the man who had owned the book – 'We know what you did in Gothenburg' – but of course nothing came of it.*

That's so much fun. I have an uncollected poem that describes my experience sitting in the train station in Albany, New York. I'm reading an Iris Murdoch paperback, which I'd bought at the Goodwill, and in the book is somebody's boarding pass. You could make up a whole novel from the itinerary. Murdoch, in fact, does that all the time.

My poem 'Searching the Scriptures' was occasioned by something a little similar. I inherited a Bible from my friend Charles Barber, who died of AIDS in 1992. I don't think that he particularly wanted me to have his Bible, but he left a lot of books to me, and his Bible was among them. As I was flipping around in it, looking up something else, a piece of paper fluttered out with a citation on it from Luke. The reference was to 'I am come to send fire on earth' – and I think that Charlie had actually annotated that. Anyway, let me not digress.

But I should get you to talk for a while about your work at the Gay Men's Health Crisis Center – the GMHC – which I guess you're starting to talk about by talking about Charles Barber. Obviously, that's something you've written about at length, in Unending Dialogue *and elsewhere, but there were a few additional things I wanted to ask you about. I'm sort of startled at the quality of the poems you were getting in this workshop, and I'm wondering if you have a theory as to why it worked as well as it did.*

It was a combination of blessed luck, one; two, I certainly did edit those poems – those are poems picked from four or five times as many. Finally, to be very politically incorrect, there was the socio-economic profile of AIDS at that time: these were educated people. Many of them had been to college. Charlie had done some graduate work at Columbia; one of the group was a minister. So it was not your average – whatever that might mean – group of people. But beyond that, the pressure of mortality on them gave the work a kind of impetus.

Anyway, I'm very happy to hear you think these poems are so good;

I think some are better than others.

Well, opening the book and flipping through it, I find poems that – if I got them from one of my students, I'd be bowled over.

Well, also, they weren't the age of our students, most of them. These poets were in their late twenties, their thirties; some of them older. Working with them seems to me now like a phase in my life when GMHC was very much the figure, and Rutgers the background. That configuration now has changed: like a long marriage, a long teaching job changes. This year I've had a wonderful experience teaching; it's been very intense. But I remember that at the time GMHC definitely trumped the classroom. Indeed, my students at Rutgers were probably getting short-changed.

There's a thing you say in 'Notes on Teaching', about how there are times when 'the classroom feels like the foreground of the teacher's life, and "real life" is what fades into a routine of obligation.' Which is maybe an even more extreme version of what you're talking about.

There you are. I'd forgotten I'd said that. It just shows, Isaac: I have very few ideas, and I repeat them.

What propelled you to start working at the GMHC, and how did that occur to you as a venue for this kind of work?

It's complicated, and I don't want to go into all the circumstances. But a couple of things: David Kalstone, who died in 1986, was one of the first people I knew and admired who died of AIDS, and I remember thinking that more should have been said about it than was. It's hard to reconstruct, but in some way AIDS frightened me and I wanted to face it. I wanted to be involved with it. And I also had begun to think, 'I need to do more in New York.' There were a lot of homeless people at that time – well, there still are, but I thought, 'I want to be engaged in something, and not just in a soup kitchen. I'd like to do what I do well.' So I set about asking the people at GMHC if I could do this, and that's how the workshop came into being.

This is something that you cover in 'The Lights Must Never Go Out', but could you describe a sort of typical workshop day? What was the atmosphere around the table, and what sort of work did you have them doing?

Well, at the beginning, as I think I say, we were in sort of a large recreation room, with cooking smells, and people doing macramé in a corner, and the workshop would just consist of me and maybe one or two other people sitting at a table. And I realized even then how strongly my whole training as a teacher or my psyche wanted a room you could go in and shut the door. Around 1990, the GMHC moved into a building, also in Chelsea, that was retrofitted for the whole purpose of GMHC, with offices and recreation space, and so the workshop would tend to go into a room in the basement and shut the door. And it was just another classroom. That felt so important to me. You go into a room, shut the door, and time stops; nothing really exists outside that classroom.

What would we do in the workshop? I would sometimes try to generate assignments for five or six weeks at a time and even give out 'syllabi', but you never knew who would be there from week to week. We were working a lot with Kenneth Koch's book *Sleeping on the Wing*, which is I think a good book for that purpose. I sometimes think that Kenneth Koch's methods tend to elicit simplistic, childish poetry, but not always.

You talk a little bit about that book in 'You Know More Than You Think You Know', your omnibus review of recent books about poetry by poets.

Right. There's a poem in *The Empty Bed* entitled 'Lower Level, Room EE', which is the number of the basement room at GMHC where we often met. Another poem in the same book is named 'Coleman 1445', after a hospital room. Outside were a Xerox machine and a coffee machine. Inside, we'd shut the door and gather around a table – which is important – and look at poems. James Turcotte, a member of the workshop, described the workshop in these terms: 'Every Thursday afternoon at three, a handful of writers faced with death sat in a circle.'

As in most workshops, people would read their poems out loud, and sometimes people would read other people's poems as well. Charlie, who had been an actor and had a wonderful sort of radio voice, read Elizabeth Bishop's 'The Moose' one day, as I recall. I wish I had that on tape.

It seems so long ago now. I don't feel good about having stopped doing it, but too many people died, many in 1992. That same year, my mother died, and I was in a constant state of mourning.

Along these lines, I thought that your preliminary question, which linked the whole workshop both to elegy and to teaching, was on target. When people call me an AIDS poet, I feel that that's an uncomfortable pigeonhole for me.

Really it seems that, in Indelible, *you're engaging elegy as a genre more than AIDS in particular, most of the time. There are the poems about the deaths of your parents, or the elegy for William Matthews, for example. And I don't know whether Paul Douglas was someone from your workshop –*

Paul Douglas was a friend of Charlie's and lived in my neighbourhood. He studied poetry at the YMHC, I think, with my friend Rachel Wetzsteon, and also showed me some work.

It seems like, in these recent elegies, you're trying to worry the question of what it is that we miss when we miss the dead. There's something of this in your uncollected piece, 'The Gleam in the Eye', where you figure loss as a sort of gradual fading from sight or notice. In 'The Last Time', that elegy for William Matthews, you write about the last time you saw him, and then ask, 'But in what sense the last?' – seeing as he still rises up from time to time in your mind's eye. Some of the people that figure in these elegies are not part of your daily routine, so they exist as sort of remembered people even when they're alive.

That's well put. In a way, the idea of writing elegies for people one doesn't know that well – it is a bit of a queasy idea. I sometimes remind myself of the woman in *Huckleberry Finn*. Huck says, 'She would whip an elegy out before they were even buried.' It's in the Grangerford and Shepherdson section: these two fancy families who are feuding. Emmeline Grangerford loves to write elegies, and she publishes them in the local paper. And I sometimes thought, 'What is it about me, what late-Victorian creepiness, that I'm so attracted to this genre?' I do think elegy is very connected to the roots of poetry. If there were no death – you know, 'Death is the mother of beauty.'

Someone said that, I believe.

It's been said. And I think I've always been better at imagining people's trouble, and imagining people's grieving, than their joy. I mean, I can imagine how it feels for anyone to lose a family member. We've all been thinking a lot about loss in the last six months anyway, but it seems to me I've always been very conscious of loss – certainly since my father's death, anyway. Whereas somebody else's joyous experience – alas, my imagination doesn't seem to work that way. I'm not very good at narrative, either. I was going to mention this dearth earlier, when we were talking about description and pictorial qualities in poems.

In some ways I'm not very curious about other people, and I'm even less curious about questions about how things work. I'm tremendously impressed, but not necessarily engaged, when prose writers, and even some poets – like Rick Kenney, with his elaborate constructions – can write about processes, and how boats work, how cars work, and how clocks work. I'm not interested in that; I'm easily bored. I'm interested in human emotions, and I think grief is probably one of the most universal. Not everybody has a talent for happiness, but as far as I can tell, everybody experiences grief.

It's really fundamental, I think. You could almost teach a plant to feel grief, in a way. If something becomes accustomed to a stimulus, and the stimulus is taken away, that's the base of grief. It's a very basic thing.

And then, childhood loss, or any kind of loss sustained when you're young, then hooks up with memory, which is the other great poetic subject. Even if you haven't lost anything else, you lose your childhood. Many people don't experience the death of a loved one until they're remarkably far-advanced in life.

Right, but you still lose each day.

You lose each day. That's right.

And a lot of time.

I was amazed at how the people in the workshop constantly faced this ticking-away of time.

Time seems to be another one of the things that you're really interested in. I can remember reading through the essay 'On Time', where you ask something like 'What are days?' or 'What are years?' ...

Poets as different as Cavafy, Emerson, and Philip Larkin have written alarming and wonderful poems about the ways we experience time. Cavafy imagines a row of candles, Emerson sees the Days as a solemn allegorical frieze, and Larkin naively asks what days are for – but 'solving that question / Brings the priest and the doctor / In their long coats /

Running over the fields.'

None of these poems is reassuring. I'm tempted to venture a pretentious generalization about poets being people who are especially obsessed by time's passage; but in fact I suspect everyone is, as they get older. I do now sense I was probably prematurely elegiac, a fact which may have had something to do with losing my father when I was seventeen. On the other hand, I think that just as young people can be more elaborately world-weary than their elders, by the same token there's no nostalgia like that of someone clinging desperately to adolescence, shrewdly sensing that adulthood, with its endless tasks and responsibilities, lies beyond. I don't know. The availability of *otium* gives us the luxury of lamenting the passage of time. When we're busier, there's less time for lamentation.

As it happens, otium *was another of the subjects I wanted to broach with you, because as I got to know your work, one of the first tropes that I saw strongly recurring was the hammock – a space in which you're reading, often, and entirely at leisure, suspended as it were above time and care. Seeing no hammocks here in New York, I take it that these poems evoke your summer lodgings in Vermont. You also have plenty of city poems, of course, but do you consider that space of summer leisure, the sense that time is somehow suspended, to be helpful or essential to your poetry, perhaps to poetry generally? Do you tend to write in Vermont more than in the city?*

I think the way it tends to work is that in Vermont I expand on hasty, rapid notes from the winter. Increasingly of late, I also do everything by hand in Vermont – one draft after another. I work at various locations: the porch; one of two tables on the lawn; a large if bat-poopy, hornet-bezoomed attic studio where there's great light and plenty of floor space to stack papers. My New York City studio in fact is a little like a suitcase I unpack in the summer. Or is my head the suitcase?

And is the process, then, one of unpacking? That seems to dovetail nicely with some things we were saying about the relation between essays and poems.

Writing poems which have somehow been stored up – getting the stuff out, spreading it, arranging and rearranging – is certainly analogous to unpacking, yes. We may like to think we travel light, but there's almost always a surprising amount packed away.

I'd like to venture a connection, if I can, to something you mentioned earlier about your workshop at the GMHC: that when you shut the door to the classroom, time stops and the outside world is suspended. That sounds familiar to me from your essay 'Notes on Teaching' and from your poem 'Pomegranate Variations', which gives a really nice sense of what your classroom might be like.

I'm struck by something you say, bravely, I think, in 'Notes on Teaching', about the 'undeniable erotics of the didactic performance', which clearly has something to do with the strange privacy of the seminar room. Are you willing to apply that general idea to 'Pomegranate Variations' in particular?

Is it so brave to mention this open secret? Anyway, call it a charge of energy.

At the very least, it's slightly taboo to speak about that energy – like, I suppose, bringing a messy fruit into a seminar room and asking the students to taste it. I don't mean to take that image too far, of course, but the pomegranate is symbolically loaded in all sorts of ways ...

What I meant to suggest, however – what I thought I heard you say – was about the classroom needing to have a door you can shut. The room has to be a space that's owned by the class, private to the class, comfortable to them.

Absolutely. Some of the doors at Rutgers Newark – they're all ugly, heavy, metal doors – some of them have little narrow windows –

You mention that in 'Pomegranate Variations': the arrow slit.

But some of them don't, at all. There's a lovely passage in Apollinaire, which I quote in my essay on teaching:

> Fermez la porte
> A double tour;
> Chacun apporte
> Son seul amour.

'Double-lock the door; everybody has their sweetie-pie in their room with them.'

Which, I want to repeat, is something rather brave to say about the class-

room. It could easily be taken the wrong way: you're not advocating a literal eros between teacher and student, only a transaction or knowledge that has to happen in private, between individuals – consenting adults, as it were.

One of the things I really enjoyed in that poem was something I've never done before or since: mentioning the students by name.
 You know, John Hollander chose 'Pomegranate Variations' for *Best Poems of the Year* – I think, 1998. And I remember I was invited to write something about it, in the contributors' notes to that volume. I remember saying at the time that the poem was written about a class I taught around 1994. It took several years to write the poem. And (talking about the relation between teaching and elegies) it was my first sort of big post-elegiac poem. Charlie Barber had died; my mother had died; everybody in *Unending Dialogue* had died by 1993 or '94. And I'd spoken at a lot of memorial services, and in a sense I'd had it with that. So it felt very life-affirming and at the same time very comfortable and safe to go on doing what I'd always done before GMHC, and indeed during it, which was teach.

And yet the text that's under discussion in the classroom – if I can call a fruit a text – is richly emblematic of the land of the dead. And also, of course, full of stains.

That's true: that indelible stain again. I was only semi-conscious of the way the stain works its way through that whole book, at the time. By the way, I'm very fond of Eavan Boland's poem, 'The Pomegranate', so I used it again this year at the beginning of my Mythology and Literature course. It's a remarkable poem: 'The best thing about the legend is / I can enter it anywhere. And have.' I put that up on the board at the beginning of my mythology class.

You say something similar to that yourself, in the poem called 'On Myth' – that one of the things about myths is that you pick them up in different circumstances, and ...

They talk to you differently.

Yes.

Which is also true of a 'classic', whatever a classic is. I'm often inspired for my own ideas, my own writing, when I'm teaching literature. I almost always learn something along the way, no matter how many times I've taught a text before.

Yes.

This is the recycling thing again, too, isn't it?

Yes and no. Coming back to a text isn't quite like recycling it. It's more like getting to know a person better. A text becomes like a person in that way: you get to know it better as you start to see what it's capable of under different circumstances.

That's a nice way of putting it, because it would be easier in a way, and less charitable, to say, 'What are the students capable of? The last class really did well with this; why don't you?' But it's much better to say, 'What is the text capable of?'

Well, I also mean that on re-encountering books I've known before, I see new aspects of them rising to new occasions. A poem I once dismissed will suddenly seem impossibly poignant. Or I go back and see lines that I've underlined, and I can't for the life of me figure out why.

John Updike has written about that important experience, and Wendy Lesser has a new book coming out about exactly that topic: re-reading *Lucky Jim* after thirty years.

And then there are other points when I think, 'How can this have been in this book all along ...'

And you never noticed.

Right.

Or, even worse, I obviously did notice once, because I underlined it, but now I've forgotten it. There's a lot of that.
 I am always struck by the triangulation that happens in the classroom: you have the text, you have the teacher, and you have the students. And although a lot of teachers of English have been poets, not all that many of them have written about teaching, partly because that triangulation

presents a problem. And at the same time, it's exciting. And it occurs to me that sometimes when I'm teaching creative writing, in a sense the triangulation doesn't happen: it's me, and the students. Because the text may, frankly, not be all that compelling. Or maybe at GMHC, the text in the room, the elephant in the living room, was AIDS.

It's also true that the texts the students bring in for workshop are often too close to being them for that triangulation to be anything but painfully acute. No matter what kind of anonymity you try to create – especially in graduate seminars, where people get to know each other better –

We don't even try.

Because you can't. – I was meaning to ask you: aside from workshops, what do you teach at Rutgers? Do they have you in the 'poet' pigeonhole? I realize I don't even know what subjects you teach.

Me neither. I'm very fortunate. I teach a great books course, called Literary Masterpieces, which –

Which is the one for which you're teaching Gilgamesh, *and things like that.*

Exactly. Homer, a little bit of Plato, a little bit of Greek tragedy. I teach writing courses at the graduate and undergraduate level; I teach American poetry at the undergraduate level, not exactly a survey. I get to make up courses. I'm very fortunate in my freedom. I haven't taught freshman English for a number of years, although I wouldn't mind teaching it *some*. Pretty daunting, especially at Rutgers Newark. In a freshman seminar once about 'The Self' – and I don't like the rubric, I had to come up with something – I taught a lot of essays, which I enjoy doing. But once I taught a creative writing class called something like 'All the Genres'. They got to do non-fiction, poetry, fiction – not that I have much right to teach fiction; it's not what I understand best.

We always have to teach a few things that we couldn't do.

Anyway, I enjoy the variety. What I'm teaching this semester – I've taught it a fair amount lately, and it changes every time I teach it – is the course I mentioned called 'Mythology and Literature'. I think the students like it. Mythology seems to provide a way to find out something they don't know, and simultaneously a way to get away from the real world, a world which is pretty painful. This course now has fifty-five people in it, which is big for a Rutgers-Newark English class.

So is there a large difference for you between teaching a creative writing course and teaching a literature course? When you teach a creative writing course, do you teach it with a lot of reading in literature?

I try to always have them do some reading, because the students as a rule have read so little. I don't believe in people writing when they've never read much. I'm sure you're familiar with many of those arguments. When I teach creative writing, I have them read. But for example, in the course I'm teaching this spring, which is for undergraduates, they want to have a workshop once a week. They really want to look at each other's work and talk about it. So I have to cram all the non-workshoppy stuff, like my lecture on metre, into the other meeting of the week.

Teaching metre: we could talk about that for hours, I'm sure. It's difficult in its way, and yet it's one of the few poetic skills that we can demonstrably teach: a line of pentameter finally either scans or doesn't. Of course, that's instruction in verse, not poetry; for students to learn how to turn a metaphor ... Well, that's a long conversation in which I would probably do too much of the talking.

Can we return, obliquely, to two questions that are vaguely related to the subject of anthologies? We've exchanged some correspondence already about what we could call the reception of your poem 'The Red Hat', which is appearing in a few anthologies or textbooks now. In particular, I'd like to get you to talk a little about the email you receive from your readers, which must be both flattering and flabbergasting.

The emails I get about 'The Red Hat' are touching, gratifying, irritating and mystifying in equal measure, or successively. I am delighted the poem is, in ways that I am less than clear about, 'out there' for readers. I am even more delighted that people enjoy it. As for their getting in touch with me, that is a human impulse facilitated by the internet, and sometimes perhaps even encouraged by their teachers. I sometimes say in my sporadic replies, 'You know, you're lucky; you wouldn't have had the luxury of asking Emily Dickinson or Keats what they were trying to say in their poems.'

I have some of the emails here, which you forwarded to me. Some of them are simply fan-mail. Those must be very gratifying.

Yes. The policeman from Douglasville, Georgia, who was doing a presentation on the poem with a classmate who worked in day care. He wrote, 'I just wanted you to know that my classmate and I are out there watching those little red hats also. Thank you for the poem.'

That's really touching.

What I find less delightful is people's apparent unwillingness to look up anything in a library or even on-line; having found my email address, they want me to do the rest.

For example: 'Where is Straus Park located[?] [I]s it near your home on West End mentioned in the poem?'

People tell me that all this means I need a website of my own. No doubt. Still, it is odd to hear that they can't find out anything about my work, or even find more of my work. How hard have they tried, I wonder? I feel like saying, 'If you go to college, there should be a library. Or even if you're on-line –'

If they can find your email address, they should be able to find your books on Amazon, at least.

But the most striking thing about the email is that they assume I have the key to my not very difficult poem, a key I will hand them. They like the poem; they are evidently moved by it. Yet some have so little confidence in their own response that they ask me 'What is the symbolism of the red hat? Was the poem written from experience? Is the main theme of separation the only theme?'

The questions sound like clumsy imitations of the questions Brooks and Warren ask the student reader in Understanding Poetry.

They are natural questions, yet they seem to me to spring from a confusion about the way poetry works, the way poets – at least this poet – arrive at decisions. There are formal queries, too: 'Why did you use the rhyme scheme you did?' and I sometimes say to people, 'I'm sorry, but poets don't work that way. At least I don't.'
    They often seem to have no confidence in their own understanding

of poetry, even though they like 'The Red Hat', presumably, because it's very accessible.

In my experience, people feel very unprepared to encounter contemporary poetry. They think that it's a very occult field, which I suppose is true about some poets, but there are certainly many contemporary poets whose books you could put into the hands of any literate person in America, and the poetry would come across. Of course, how one gets the poems into their hands is another difficult question.
    Deciding on a rhyme scheme isn't something one could explain, anyway. It comes mostly by intuition or the sense of touch. I know there are times, in thinking about a yet-unwritten poem, when I understand: this has to be in triplets; or in stanzas of some heft, maybe eight or nine lines apiece. But most of the time it is a process of finding out.

Definitely. And at least for me, the process is extremely intuitive, so that it's hard to reconstruct. When I'm writing well, I write fast, and afterwards I can't really remember how I arrived at my decisions. But also, I've become a much better reviser, and, in the past few years, a lot of my work has been by way of revising old poems. Almost always the old poem seems flabby and wordy to me. So I take tucks in it, but in the process, other ideas may occur to me, which then expand it. I have an essay on revision where I talk a bit about that.

What anthology does 'The Red Hat' appear in, to find its way into so many hands?

It's actually in three anthologies. I don't know if that's kosher. It's in *Rebel Angels*, which you referred to in one of your preliminary questions. It's in the ninth and tenth or tenth and eleventh editions of *Perrine's Sound and Sense*, which I think is a very good book. It was taught to me when I was in high school, so it's a real honour for me to be in it now. Are you familiar with Perrine?

It sounds familiar enough to convince me I also had it as a text in high school, or thereabouts.

Perrine died some years ago, and the editor is now Thomas Arp, and a whole lot of other people, but the title of the book, if you look it up on Amazon, is now *Perrine's Sound and Sense*. It's quite a good book, on a number of different levels, and it has a mini-anthology in back, and that's where 'The Red Hat' is.

It's also in a not terribly good textbook, the title of which escapes me – a textbook where they're attempting to teach how to read poetry, maybe how to write it, how to write about it: trying to do too many things at once and doing none of them very well.

Also, the people who are responding to 'The Red Hat' don't tell me where they encountered it. I think they were given photocopies, of it.

Quite possibly. I don't know that Rebel Angels *is being assigned in courses a whole lot, although I guess it's in a second printing now. (I could tell, because my students' copies this term look different and feel different from the one I have.)*

The contents haven't changed?

No, it's only a second printing, not a new edition. The book looks and feels slightly different: cover a little lighter, the pages a little more flexible.

The whole issue of anthologies is something else we could talk about.

I know it's something you've been thinking about, as a general subject, recently. I wanted to ask you particularly about anthologies as they are used to define or articulate poetic 'movements' – in particular, Rebel Angels *as it relates to the 'New Formalism' in America*

I ask because there you had a short piece in The Kenyon Review *in 1991, in which you seemed somewhat ambivalent about the project or 'movement' that was starting to be called The New Formalism; then you were brought under its umbrella by the* Rebel Angels *anthology a few years later.*

I think I've gotten maybe a little bit braver about my ambivalence. I'm almost always wishy-washy; I always see two sides of an issue. And a lot of things that were being said by New Formalists struck me as either painfully obvious, or else just inaccurate. I mean, it wasn't new: there always was a formalism. And to the degree that it was a self-proclaimed New Formalism, it was suspect as a movement in all kinds of ways I hardly need to go into. They have to do with self-promotion of individual poets.

As far as being then brought under its umbrella, all last year at the New York Public Library I was working on a project on anthologies, some of which has recently seen the light of day, by the way, in the AWP organ, *The Writer's Chronicle.*

One thing I was able to glean from my research was that a great many poets, especially when they're young, are so thrilled to be in anthologies, they don't ask any questions. Especially if it's a real, non-vanity anthology, and you're not paying to be in it. An editor invites you to be in an anthology; you even get paid a little. It doesn't occur to you to say, 'Who else is in this anthology?'

I once talked to Mark Doty about that. I don't know Mark well, but I think of him as a very professional, canny, and conscientious person, and I believe he said he rarely even remembered who was in anthologies with him.

I respect Mark Jarman and David Mason, and in some ways I like *Rebel Angels*, but of course one disagrees with individual choices, and then there's the larger issue of the New Formalism. I'm just as guilty as anyone else of appearing under rubrics about which I have mixed feelings.

There are things I've noticed about the New Formalism, from reading essays about it by various poets: first, that no one seems to be happy with the name, except perhaps the person who coined it. Second, that many of the people who are in that anthology are not people I'd think of as being aggressively formalist, on the one hand, or likely to join up with the formalist crowd, on the other hand. Andrew Hudgins is writing in metre, for example, but I have a hard time picturing him wanting to be a part of this 'movement' as such.

And I'd hazard a guess that the same thing is true, in a different way, of you and your work. Certainly your work doesn't seem to need a New Formalist banner to justify its formal practice.

Or to piggyback or hitchhike a ride with such an anthology in order to get into print in the first place. Although most of the poets in *Rebel Angels* already had reputations.

It is an odd anthology, in who it includes and maybe who it leaves out, but you know what? Oddness is simply the way anthologies *are.* And then you look back at an anthology twenty years later, and you think, 'How bizarre that that person's there.' Or, 'How bizarre that that person isn't there.' But usually, so many people are *not* in a given anthology that it's odder to think who *is.*

Going back to my piece in *Kenyon Review*: it's an ill-tempered little piece, and I hold no great brief for it. I think it temporizes in certain ways. And I think a few people were annoyed by it, but that also goes with the territory of the New Formalism. People seem to get very annoyed by what other people say.

Well, it's a weirdly politicized segment of contemporary poetry. It seems to me that anyone who comes out against writing in form seems to be making really strange assumptions about –

About what formalism is, or –

About what form is, in a poem. And yet at the same time, people who come out to say that poetry will be more accessible to the common reader if everyone starts writing in metre and rhyme – that's a slightly crazy assertion, too. It's not merely the sound of poems that make them accessible or inaccessible. People love e. e. cummings, or they used to. And some of Hart Crane's wildest inscrutabilities are in metre.

Well, the sound of a poem makes it memorable, memorizable, singable. But I am by temperament – after you get to be fifty, and you keep on getting older, you earn the right to say things like, 'I'm not a curious person,' or 'I this, I that' – really averse to making blanket statements about what poetry is, or should be, or does. That's why it's really much more educational to write reviews. You have to keep seeing what the zeitgeist is tossing up.

If you were to ask me about trends that I see, I'd say I learn more by doing a roundup review of ten new books of poems, many of which I've seen in manuscript, or I've heard of the authors, or I've met them, or they've applied for something that I've judged, so they're out there. You feel you're getting a little glimpse of poetry as it's manifesting in this moment. But if you're somewhere in the empyrean, and you say, 'Poetry is this' or 'Poetry should do that' – well, I don't presume to have that kind of authority.

Not that I don't have opinions, and reactions, and a certain testiness as I get older, but I prefer not to make categorical statements about poetry.

Sure. And it seems clear that, if nothing else, the market will bear a large variety of different things called 'poetry', and none of them is ever going to be widely popular or successful in the way that a movie or even a home video-game is going to be successful.

One of the interesting things, actually, as a reviewer, or a teacher, is to see which work looks as if it's going to turn into something else: Mary Gordon began her career as a poet, before Elizabeth Hardwick told her to write fiction. And fiction turned out to be much more lucrative – surprise, surprise.

Yes, fancy that.

Plenty of writers might begin as poets and move off in some other direction. I've met my share of young playwrights at Sewanee, and I think poetry and plays do have a kind of relationship. I'm not so sure about poetry and fiction. But one of the more poorly edited and conceived volumes I'm reviewing now is by a young poet who doesn't seem sure she's a poet. I think she thinks maybe she's a journalist, or she could write a short story, or a satire. But she perhaps thinks poems are easier.

At the Yale Series of Younger Poets I see a half a dozen or a dozen manuscripts every year that consist of sixty-four pages of 'prose poems'.

There's a lot of that going around, too.

Certainly there are a few that are interesting to read, and actually, in a way, you could make a case that Kafka's short pieces are prose poems by today's definitions. But what do you get, I wonder, from calling them 'prose poems'?

Somebody said – I want to say it's John Ashbery, but I don't think so; he's written prose poems himself – 'I don't understand what prose poems are. I don't trust them.' It might be Merrill. Anyway, the work I'm doing in reviewing these new books is very much like the work you're doing in weeding out as you read manuscripts for the Yale Younger Poets.

Yes, in a way, although a reviewer sees the results of the process.

These books I'm reviewing are the people who have made it, and usually you can see why. In a few cases you can't; you think, 'Oh my God, what was the competition like for this one?'

Working for the Series, I get a vague sense of the trends our young, un-

published poets are following: Ashbery imitators were common for a while, then a batch of Jorie Graham followers; now there seems to be a vogue for certain kinds of humour ...

Did you see the cartoon in the New Yorker *that had two people talking, and one of them is saying, 'I like poems, but only when they're funny.'*

Well, Donald Hall says somewhere – I think it's in the introduction to his *Oxford Book of American Children's Verse* – that in the nineteenth century, poetry for children was expected to be didactic, and full of death and moralizing. And now it has to be funny. It has to be Shel Silverstein: sort of cartoony, or otherwise children won't like it.

Actually I think the cartoon has to do with a trend in poetry for adults, or a trend in its publicly visible manifestations: our current laureate Billy Collins, I guess, or Mark Strand's Blizzard of One, *maybe. But what I meant to say was that my time in the trenches at the Series doesn't really give me any ability to predict beyond this year's fashions. (What a bizarre mixed metaphor.)*

You had a short essay for The Writer *in which you list for the hopeful writer what poems have done in the past, and what they can do: they can insult, they can elegize, they can praise, they can describe or draw portraits or tell jokes, I suppose. But, as you say there, if the young writer has some of these goals, might he or she really want to be writing a play or drawing a cartoon?*

I wanted to ask you about any sense you might have of what's next: the possible genres, possible goals, for American poetry in the next ten or twenty years.

You mentioned something like that in one of your preliminary questions, but I think I may have misread it to ask, 'What poems do *I* want to do?'

Well, there's that, too. Either or both. I guess I had asked what you imagine yourself writing, but I'm also curious about possible trends, and what the auguries are.

As I said earlier, I have no narrative talent. I couldn't write a short story if you put a gun to my head. But I wouldn't mind writing a play. I can't do plots, but if somebody provided a plot I might enjoy writing dialogue. In terms of what I do with poetry, the idea of the versified essay is probably what most appeals to me. I could quite easily get to the point where I might write a book review in blank verse, or something.

And it's not entirely far from the kind of verse essays that you're already writing, whether or not they're being called verse essays: poems like 'Change is the Stranger' or 'The Hermit'.

I was recently invited to a retirement dinner for Robert Fagles, the translator, who was my teacher at Princeton. I've been asked to do a brief tribute, and I thought I might do it in verse. I've gotten lazier as I've gotten older, about this kind of almost commissioned thing, but I want to praise him, and to praise him in a particularized way. So. Certainly eulogy, or elegy: all of these things fit so nicely into verse.

Other than that, verse drama? There's a little group in New York City called Verse Theater of Manhattan who are trying to revive verse drama, and they put on Christopher Fry, and they put on my translation of the *Helen*; I applaud that.

The new director of the poetry programme at the 92nd Street Y, David Yezzi, is very interested in where poetry meets theatre or meets music, where these things interface.

That must be something that you think about and talk about a lot, at home, since your husband is a composer: the intersection, easily misunderstood I think, between poetry and music. Certainly when poets have tried to bring blues or jazz to their poetry, it works best metaphorically, rather than in any attempt to imitate music directly. And when I hear a poem set to music – in operatic melody, for example – by a composer, the transposition often ignores the music of the poem, or the 'sentence sound', and ruins the poem in the process.

Well, a musical setting often doesn't do much for the poem, though I don't think it can ruin the poem.

Well, it doesn't ruin the poem that's still there on the page.

Right. I'm very familiar with this, because I know many composers, and I've been to artists' colonies a lot, so I've had my own share of poems set, and I'm often less than thrilled with the results. I think it's wonderful that composers want to pay a lot of attention to poetry, but sometimes they're a little lazy about it. Some say to me, or to any poet they meet, 'Oh, you're a poet: you must know a good poem for me to set.' They don't really want to have to do the homework. But nevertheless, if you're wanting to celebrate the work of a poet, and you have an event, and the event includes some such settings, I think that's fine. It's just one other way of approaching or performing the poem.

I don't mean to say that it can't be done, only that it seems much more complicated than a first, facile understanding might suggest – 'Poems have sound and rhythm: that makes them like music.' You rarely see someone trying to make things go the other way, for example. Very, very few lyricists, at least for popular music, care whether their lyrics will bear up on the page the way poems do, and with good reason. There are different demands on a listener's attention in the different media. This is why a blues lyric can be utterly heartbreaking as sung and look like total foolishness on the page.

They look simple-minded.

And for the same reason, it has been hard – I think Hayden Carruth talks about this unattainable goal – to get the effects of blues lyrics in a poem written upon the page. But I'm riding my own hobbyhorse here, so let me dismount.
We were talking about verse drama: I know that the Paris Review *has a prize for verse drama; I think Karl Kirchwey won it with his version of* Alcestis *a few years ago.*

That's right. But I wouldn't even get as far as writing one, because I don't have any plot. I'm not even good at dramatic monologue, so why do I say drama?
Nevertheless, at Sewanee one year, the playwright Horton Foote was very kind about some of my poems: he seemed to feel that I had dramatic talent, but he wasn't quite able to convey to me what he meant. And then I alarmed him by saying, 'Well, Horton, suppose I wrote a play; what should I do with it?' And he said, 'Don't you have an agent?' I said, 'No,' and that ended that conversation. I didn't want to bother the poor man.

Why would a poet have an agent?

Well, some poets do. Wishful thinking, I think.

The poet would have to be making actual money from poetry, for the agent to skim from.

Poets have agents because they – the poet or the agent – hope that the poet *will* make money, so the agent tries to get the poet to write a biography, or a series of popular articles ... It becomes very convoluted and silly.

The essay 'You Know More Than You Think You Do' – that round-up review of books about poetry by poets – seems to me to be dealing in my jaundiced way with what a lot of poets at mid-career or later are doing. They're saying, 'There's a problem with poetry in this culture, so I'm going to write a book and make it better.' I suppose that's one of the things I might do, but I resist doing it.

How would you define that problem?

Oh, boy. 'She took a bite of her sandwich.' I haven't tried to define it to myself. Some of the symptoms are evinced by that email that amused you so: the one asking for a 'translation' of 'The Red Hat'.

Right.

But the whole topic is finally tedious. People have been bouncing this around, at least since Dana Gioia's essay, 'Can Poetry Matter?' or Joseph Epstein's before that. I mean that, no, the culture doesn't value poetry, but there are many writing programmes, and there are many poetry readings, and there are a lot of poets out there. All these things are true. I don't know that I can make sense of it. I think there's more of a poetry scene, or scenes, in America than in a lot of places.

It would be hard to imagine the alternative. Would there be television shows about poetry? About poets? About ...?

Well, I suppose the big thing we're avoiding is the whole medium of the internet. More and more people just post their poems.

Do you think the internet is going to change the way people see, discover, or read poetry? I don't just mean on-line journals like Slate *or* Blackbird, *or sites like 'poems.com', but the nearly infinite prospects for 'self-publication'. If you're not inclined to prognosticate, maybe there's some way in which you can sense the internet already affecting your own work? I know you've written about the metaphor of the 'worldwide web'.*

One thing I'm too much of a dinosaur to know is whether, when people see poems they like on-line, they download them and keep tangible copies – the kind of thing you post on your refrigerator – or leave them floating in cyberspace. I'd suspect the former, but maybe that's wishful thinking.

The more interesting problem is the aesthetics of on-line publishing. Does the airy whoosh of material mean that people will actually read and write differently, or are already doing so? I have general instincts about this but no real information, let alone facts and figures. Much poetry I see is loose, wordy, spontaneous, and unmemorable. Word processing should make revising easier, but that's not necessarily the way it's used.

That's a good catalogue of the vices of electronically facilitated writing – the problems of an email culture, as it were: spontaneity of a temporary sort, looseness, verbosity. Are there virtues in this kind of writing, as well, or does the word processor become an enemy to poetry as soon as it's anything more than a typewriter?

I have no magisterial thoughts about how computers might actually serve to improve the way writers write, as distinguished from changing how we read and possibly degrading how we write. The speed of the keyboard has helped me when I've drafted prose as well as revised it; I'm a fast if inaccurate typist and the word processor has helped my fingers keep pace with my thoughts. This speed is fine, I'd say, so long as one doesn't mistake (as students so often do) the clean-looking page for anything but the draft it is. I suspect many writers would say the same.

As for poetry, I can only be empirical and say I usually compose several drafts, by hand, then word-process it and print out the results, which I then revise by hand, repeating the process as often as needed: three, five, twelve times. More manual versions help (that is, for each typed version I may do two or three by hand), but then I periodically need the typed page to see (and in an odd way to hear) what I've written. I should add that sometimes in summer and once at an artists' colony, lacking a decent printer, I've written many, many drafts by hand, put them on disk, and not until I got home printed up the results, which were often (as they say) camera-ready copy – a pleasant surprise. 'The Gleam in the Eye', for example, was composed this way one summer, epigraph and all. I remember tracking down the epigraph from *Our Town* at the local library.

If my aim were always speed, looseness, and spontaneity, on the one hand, or a hard gem-like flame, on the other – in other words, if I always knew what effect I was after – then this question would be easier to answer, and the poems would be easier to write. Still, I like the unpredictability and variability of the process.

Granted, then, that you're not always sure about the goals of an individual poem, what would you say are the characteristics you value in your work more generally? What are you aiming at?

For the individual poem, I often don't know till the thing is done. Both Robert Frost and my neighbour, the poet Jane Cooper, have written of the ache, the uneasiness that gives rise to poems or that poems address. Poems come from both loss and plenitude; they capture, or retrieve, or enact. Do I bear this in mind when I sit down to write? Of course not. A dream may set me off, or a scrap of overheard conversation, or something I see or remember, or a reaction of irritation or amazement. There's Frost again: 'When they ask about inspiration, I tell them it's mostly animus.'

As far as the how, as opposed to the what, in my work: I want weight, authority, precision, cadence – not a minimalist precision, but a clean line, even in longer or more meandering poems, so that the reader isn't lost. Syntax and clarity can't be sacrificed on the altar of feeling. Weight, clarity, rhythm: these can be improved with revision.

***

We left off talking in April of 2002, and at the time the most recent of your books was Indelible, *which we discussed. It's now 2005, and you have a new book,* Laws, *and are pretty far into writing the next one.*

I'm not certain about the publication dates, but I have two books forthcoming from David Robert Books in Cincinnati. It's a small press; they publish good people like Dolores Hayden and John Talbot. There is a book of poems called *The River of Forgetfulness*, which will be coming out sometime in 2006, and a collection of essays which surprised me by its length, called *Classics*, which I think will probably be out some time in 2007.

I've been re-reading Laws, *and one of the things I see coming up over and over again – and it's related to the title of the book – is your announced inclination in the book to talk not about yourself but about other people, and what you observe in other people. In the third section of 'Three Mirror Stages', you say that you meet your own reflection in the mirror now the same way that you would acknowledge someone across the room at a party, with a wink –*

'But as one steers through a crowded party / As much escaping A as seeking B, / I would rather look at someone else.'

And that seems to be an intention in the book as a whole, which I think starts to give the book its title, because you're not speaking about the sort of laws that get enacted in Washington, but observed laws, like the laws of thermodynamics or Murphy's Law.

Definitely laws that are observed: laws of human beings in time, of human development. And, although it's true that in the opening poem, 'The Chorus', I say, 'my poems used to play the heroine, "me me me"', it seems to me that quite a few of the poems in this book are still in the first person, so I'm not sure how successful I've been in avoiding it. When I come into the poems, however, as I often do, it might be more in terms of my own falling into line with different laws.

Or as an observer, gathering evidence or deducing patterns. We had talked about your interest in the verse essay, and I wonder if that line of thinking intersects with this one, or whether they're really the same line of thought after all? These are poems that are about trying to adduce something, trying to work your way toward the knowledge of a pattern.

I would like to think that my poems aren't getting more prosaic and sententious, but at the same time, they are more and more ratiocinative. And by the same token, some of the material I cover in my essays is material that I might once have covered in poetry.

    It seems that Robert Pinsky is moving these days toward the role of 'man of letters', away from just being a 'poet', and I feel a similar pull. It reminds me of what Auden did: it's not that he ever stopped writing poetry, but Auden was too *smart*, and too well read, to pour it all into the narrow spigot of poetry.

That's well put. There are ideas that belong in a more discursive medium, one that's less straitened –

I don't mean to put poetry down. If we were living in the age of Lucretius, I could write a five-thousand-line poem about memory or history or science, but we're not living in that age. I feel drawn to prose non-fiction; if I'm asked to talk about something, I often will write a short, short essay, and it has a certain weight.

Toward the end of his life, James Merrill would be asked to write an essay; he'd be asked to contribute to a collection of something. And he'd usually write a paragraph, or a page. He was pleased to be asked, but he felt that what he had to say didn't need to take up that much room. And every word was golden.

If you turn to prose when you feel like you have more authority on a subject, then are your poems necessarily more exploratory, and less certain? I suppose that's another way of saying 'ratiocinative': you're thinking something through in a poem, rather than speaking about something you already understand.

But it's also not the case, in essays, that I'm speaking from a place of conclusion. I usually write – anything at all – to figure out what I think. And that's true of the essay as well.

That's what the word 'essay' is supposed to mean, after all, and that's probably what I mean, more than anything else, when I talk about certain of your poems as verse essays.

I was never that much of a narrative poet, but I think I was once more of a lyric poet, and I am more of an observer now. There's a poem called 'The Departure', where

> Later a cooling curls the corners up.
> One finds a peaceful perch from which (as in
> a nineteenth-century novel or a story
> by Katherine Mansfield, matrons at a dance
>
> sit on little gilded chairs against
> the wall and watch their daughters waltz) to view
> the widening gap between the self
> and all it recently so fiercely wanted.

So if I'm sitting on this little gilded chair, like a kind of chaperone at the dance of life, am I seeing the younger generation, as in this story by Katherine Mansfield called 'Her First Ball' – I haven't read it since I was fourteen, but obviously it made an impression on me – which is one way we can stand to get older, because we see these things that are simply true – or, as I see that I say in 'The Departure', am I just watching my younger self? It's an interesting question: when older people sit and watch the spectacle of life, are they watching as anthropologists, or are they watching their younger selves, or are they watching like an explorer on another planet?

This image takes different forms in Laws. *There are poems in which you're watching strangers, or friends, and there are other poems, like 'The Compact', where you're looking back at your younger self, and even your younger self looking in the mirror.*

Yes, indeed. There's a funny story about 'The Compact': I got a very nice emailed paper from a student at Purdue whose instructor had seen 'The Compact' in *American Scholar* and assigned his class to write about it. She wrote very well about the image of the mirror but the climax of her paper really was that 'this poem is about facing imminent death': apparently, by the time you've been out of high school for forty years, you're on the brink of the grave. And of course, she was twenty: that's how it looked to her.

Shall we say that what we've been talking about is that these are poems of middle age.

I think that in the book the question of middle age is strongly connected to the question of observing other people. But that choice to observe, rather than to try to make yourself the hero of the poem, is something that I admire in poets whether or not they are middle-aged. I wish that my students, for example, could take up this sort of perspective, or that more first books of poetry would be less lyric and more ruminative.

Maybe you have to be middle-aged to get there. I think it's too bad it took me so long. But a certain kind of detachment is hard-won. I'm thinking of something like Craig Raine's 'A Martian Sends a Postcard Home': that almost Brechtian alienation effect, so that what you're seeing on the stage draws attention to its own artificiality. I'm almost deliberately drawing a frame and saying, 'I'm sitting here, watching the world go by.' It could easily teeter into self-pity or boringness – you know: Rachel the old philosopher, sitting on a cracker barrel. That does not appeal to me at all.

Also, in fairness to the young poets, I have plenty of problems with many of the first books I read, but I think the centrality of 'I' is natural.

And I often actually don't like the ways in which writers try to escape from it, by writing in the second person, for example, or by making every single poem about (and spoken by) Rosa Parks or Simone Weil or Joan of Arc or whoever it may be.

In some ways, of course, it's impossible to escape that first-person pronoun. You're the person who's writing. Even if the first person who's speaking is Mr Spectator, there's still some first person guiding the observations, and you wouldn't want to deny that in verse, because the expectation is that a poem is written by someone, after all.

I wonder whether some of the condition of being the chaperone, sitting against the wall and watching the dance, might come from the fact that – well, I don't know whether this is true for you, but most of the people that I interact with, in a given week, are my students – increasingly, most of the people I see are younger and more active than I am.

You know, as far as being the chaperone goes, and sitting on the side while the kids dance, in a way it's the opposite: there are fifty students there, and they're sitting there watching *me* dance.

Sitting on the sidelines more resembles my experience just walking down the street and noticing that most people I see are younger than I am. Maybe as I get older I'm just becoming a better observer. I try to listen better. I don't know. Does this usually happen in the middle age of a lyric poet? I don't know.

I'm interested in the way that observation becomes, not really a kind of introspection, but more a looking back at yourself, through the world, or by means of the world, as in the image of a mirror, which comes up a couple of times. Of course, it's a kind of historical mirror, or a memory mirror: you don't wind up looking at your current self, the sort of lyric 'I', but instead it's a kind of retrospect. It's in part because one of the things you're most interested in observing is other people – you're not a poet who is interested in landscapes or, as you said, in 'how things work'.

In some ways I'm very incurious, but I'm not incurious about people. One of the things about my first book, *Slow Transparency*, or my chapbook *Starting From Troy*, is that I was living in Greece, where it was very beautiful, and some of that beauty made its way into the poems, but the poems weren't the best vehicles for that beauty. The poems read to me, now, as over-decorated, over-written, and too much about the azure sky and sunset – and it's not that there's *no* observation of people there, too, but I'm now far more interested in the way human beings function.

If the turn to poetry is a move away from the sort of landscape depiction that is more natural in painting, some of the observation and reasoning that you're doing in your poems now seems like the kind of thing that many people would cast in fiction. I know you admire Mansfield and Austen. I wonder: do you have any new inclination in that direction?

As I've often said, I don't have a narrative gift. I'm not good at making up characters and having them interact. But there are two things that I can do that fiction writers should perhaps be able to do: I write prose quite well, and I like to listen to and to reproduce people's voices.

Sometimes my poems have a lot of overheard or quoted words in them, in different ways: 'Pronoun Variations' has those obnoxious Christmas letters, for example, which kind of set me off. 'Reading *The Princess*' has the technician who was taking my blood saying (about Tennyson), 'A little / of *that* would be enough, I would imagine.' 'Basic Human Dread' is a conversation. There's quite a lot of that. There are many references to things that people have said to me – in 'Field Notes on Younger Siblings', for example – even if I'm not quoting them verbatim.

If you were a novelist interested in these laws of human conduct, it seems like you might work in the opposite direction: in your poems, you observe and then draw conclusions; a novelist who is interested in the same things might have a conclusion in mind, and then create a narrative that led to it –

Working backwards? I really don't know if a novelist would have a conclusion in place or not.

Maybe I'm being unfair to novelists. I suppose that they must also begin mostly with observation, speculation, retrospection.

I was giving a small reading at the New School last week. One of the poems I read there was 'The Compact', and I had occasion to expand a little on the line, 'Those uphill rides were forty years ago.' (They were forty years ago when I wrote the poem.) Forty years, when you get to be my age – I'll be fifty-seven next week – forty years is a number that you can't get away from. When Kerry and Bush were debating, Kerry would say, 'Forty years ago, in Vietnam, I did this.' And the Kennedy assassination was forty years ago. Goodman, Cheney, and Schwerner were murdered in Mississippi forty years ago. Everything seems to have happened forty years ago. And then the number turns up in one of my favourite poems by Thomas Hardy, 'Channel Firing'; it turns up in 'High Windows', by Philip Larkin.

It's a round number big enough to sound like a milestone, but small enough so that people actually can remember that far in the past.

And can remember without being on the point of death, as that student at Purdue thought. I mean, I can remember being a fifteen-year-old powdering her nose on a bus, and I can remember that without being a hundred, without remembering the Civil War.

I'm in the situation now where I'm remembering things that took place in the year that my students were born, or a little earlier, as part of my 'adult' life.

I'm just about on the cusp where my students are either the age of my son, who was born in 1984, or younger than my son. It moves right along.

I've just finished teaching a book that was written in 1984, and consequently has all of these Cold-War fears about the Russians and nuclear war in it, and I have to inform my students – not remind them, but tell them for the first time – that back in that ancient decade, around the time of their birth, we were still actually worried that some other nation might trigger a nuclear war. Today's college students seem to have very little access to any cultural moment before the one they're living in.

That's one of the challenges and delights and horrors of teaching. I've been teaching *Don Juan*, which is a lot of fun, and one of the students said, 'Did they like intelligent women then?' And I said, 'First of all, you're talking as if they were all tyrannosaurus rexes. Has human nature changed that much in two hundred years?'
    I used to think of myself as a stubbornly nonhistorical poet. But if you live long enough, you're trapped into being historical! Another poem that I talked about at the New School is 'The Gaze', which ends with the word *historical*, and which pulls together Cavafy, James Merrill, 9/11, and 'The Shield of Achilles'. Experience becomes public and historical. It doesn't just belong to you: it belongs to your whole city, or your whole

generation.

That touches on another bit of Auden, too: the notion that suffering is always going on off in the corners, away from the drama of another life, 'While someone else is eating or opening a window or just walking dully along. ... / The dogs go on with their doggy life.'

Right. I've been thinking a lot about Auden, and one reason he has lasted so well is that he keeps speaking directly to us.

These little bits of Auden that we keep using in our conversations are such concise, apt and wise statements, that by themselves, even out of the poems, they work a little like poems, or like maxims, or magical formulae. There's something very true and very certain about his best lines.

Another form this recognition of laws can take, or this kind of observer-of-the-world-of-life: since I am a reader I observe texts, too, and I quote from them, as many, many poets do. It doesn't even seem even like incredible bookishness; it just seems like the only way I can make sense of things.

People become poets because they're interested in words; words are a large part of the world that you observe.

In 'Headlines in The National Herald', where I'm reading the Greek paper, and I talk about 'the double pleasure recognition / affords', I know the word that I see in this Greek headline, and the word clues me in to Cavafy's poem – it's like an internet search, if you like – and then the headlines and the poem sort of triangulate, though I don't use that word, and I seem to need words to remind me that history happens. The headlines and the poem are reminders: wars happen; prisoners are taken.
  And talk about looking at things backwards. Do you see where I'm coming from there?

The word itself reminds you of a story that reminds you of the world. One of the things that you get from spending time with literature is a really strong sense of the historical quality of the words themselves, and the language itself. So that we hear, as we talk, lines of Auden or lines of Cavafy, or bits of Herodotus – not just the etymology of the words, but the past utterances of those words and phrases. If that's the case, then the language itself has, just as physical things do, that smudge of human use or human contact that we were talking about when we spoke about Indelible: *the thumbprint; that thing that Hardy is so good at describing, the wear on an object that has been used for a generation or two. Of course, words only show that kind of use if you know their history.*

And in those Greek newspaper headlines, as I passed my local newsstand that morning, I saw a word that means something like *hostage* or *prisoner of war* (this was during the Kosovo bombing); I knew that the word was a word in ancient Greek, and I had to go look it up in the lexicon. To think that Herodotus used exactly the same word is actually quite a mind-blower, especially because there's no one word equivalent in English: *prisoner of war* is about as close as we come.

It makes you historical. This business about 'I need language to make the world seem real' is what 'Demeters' is about.

> The desire to be physically close to the beloved
> turns out to be a lesson learned so well
> or so intuitive in the first place
> it didn't need to be repeated.
> Except it did, apparently it did,
> lifelong. ...
>
> To force me to pay attention,
> life needed poetry. And poetry needed life
> in order to flow like blood
> through any woman's veins.

Timothy Steele

photo courtesy of
Barian

A NOTE ON TIMOTHY STEELE

Timothy Steele was born in 1948 in Burlington, Vermont. He was educated at the local public, or state, schools from which he moved on to Stanford University. He received his PhD from Brandeis where that rigorous teacher and poet J. V. Cunningham became a powerful influence on his own development as a poet. He was appointed a Wallace Stegner Fellow and Jones Lecturer in Poetry at Stanford before moving in 1977 to Los Angeles, where he now serves as a professor of English at the city's California State University campus. He has won many awards and honours, amongst them: a Guggenheim Fellowship; a Peter I. B. Lavan Younger Poets Award from the Academy of American Poets; the Los Angeles PEN Center's Award for Poetry, and a Commonwealth Club of California Medal for Poetry.

He has been mistakenly associated, even identified by some, with the 'New Formalists', but his interest in, advocacy and use of traditional form began much earlier than the stirrings of that amorphous grouping. His own talents in this direction were probably influenced and encouraged early on by the powerful practice of Cunningham and the ghostly ambience of Yvor Winters. Steele's proclivity has always been to use the full expressive resources of traditional metre; his characteristic registers usually hover round the plain style found, for example, in Ben Jonson's lyric and epigrammatic verse. Steele would subscribe to the Wintersian idea of the importance of intelligence in the making of accessible verse, reason holding the reins of emotion. Yet his work does not feel as constricted as Winters often sounds since there is also an underlying influence from Frost which can ease the rhythmic and emotional advance of a poem of Steele's. In *Uncertainties and Rest* (Baton Rouge, Louisiana, 1979), and *Sapphics against Anger* (New York, 1986), there is a passion and wit delivered with an underlying authority and control in dealing with Vermont landscapes and Californian scenes. But, unlike so many contemporaries, Steele is not averse to dealing more abstractly with topics such as culture, faith and friendship. Also included in these books are some nicely judged love poems, not to mention epigrams of lapidary power, the form favoured by his old mentor J. V. Cunningham. *The Color Wheel* (Baltimore, Maryland), carrying much of the same conviction, appeared in 1994. A selected poems, *Sapphics and Uncertainties: Poems 1970-1986*, appeared from The University of Arkansas Press, Fayetteville, in 1995. His most recent collection is *Toward the Winter Solstice* (Athens, Ohio, 2006), which prompted *Booklist*'s Ray Olson to describe him as 'so technically adroit that he could write about anything and produce a poem repeatedly rewarding for music and shapeliness alone, and subject matter be damned.'

Steele's prose criticism has had considerable influence, particularly in America, not least on the previously mentioned, so-called New Formalists. *Missing Measures: Modern Poetry and the Revolt against Meter* (Fayetteville, Arkansas/London, 1990), is a scholarly work which closely argues the case for the traditional approach to metrics and form. Wilbur wrote of it: 'If it has not the slam-bang simplicity of polemic it has something better: it is patiently evidential and well-nigh incontestable.'

Missing Measures was followed by another prose work, *All the Fun's in How You Say a Thing: An Explanation of Meter and Versification* (Athens OH, 1999), designed to explain metrics in detail for those now brought up without that once traditional knowledge. Steele has also edited *The Music of His History: Poems for Charles Gullans on His Sixtieth Birthday* (Florence, Kentucky, 1989) and, with introduction and commentary, *The Poems of J. V. Cunningham* (Athens, Ohio, 1997).

A note on Cynthia Haven

Cynthia L. Haven was born in Detroit and educated at the University of Michigan Ann Arbor, where she studied with the late Joseph Brodsky and earned two prestigious Avery Hopwood Awards for Literature. After receiving her university degree, she moved to London and worked at *Vogue, Index on Censorship*, and a short-lived Third-World newsweekly on Fleet Street, the *World Times*.

Currently, she is a literary critic at the *San Francisco Chronicle* and writes regularly for the *Times Literary Supplement*, the *Washington Post Bookworld*, the *Los Angeles Times Book Review* and the *Cortland Review*. Her work has also been published in *Civilization, Commonweal,* the *Kenyon Review*, and the *Georgia Review*. Her interview with Thom Gunn appeared in the *Georgia Review*, spring-summer issue, 2005. She has been affiliated with Stanford University for many years, and is a regular contributor to its magazine.

Recipient of over a dozen literary and journalistic awards, she has written several non-fiction books. Her most publications are *Joseph Brodsky: Conversations* (University Press of Mississippi, Jackson, Mississippi, 2003/Adelphi Edizioni, Milan, 2005), *Peter Dale in Conversation with Cynthia Haven* (BTL, London, 2005) and *Czeslaw Milosz: Conversations*, (University Press of Mississippi, Jackson, Mississippi, 2006).

Timothy Steele in conversation with Cynthia Haven

Let me begin with a confession. In preparing for this interview, I read your poetry through in pretty much one go, beginning to end. While I've always been an admirer, ever since we met at a reading in 1986, it was the first chance I've had in years to read and think about your poetry quite separately from your scholarship. Many of the poems are really stellar, and I went to bed quite enchanted with the opus. The problem: your scholarship is remarkable as well. Do you get tired of answering questions about your scholarship when you are, after all, first and foremost a poet?

You're right, the poetry comes first and foremost. But I don't resent questions about the scholarship; I'm grateful for the attention it's received.

In a 1995 interview, you noted that you initially avoided the scholarly works, because, you said, they 'impinged so closely on writing verse.' Do you feel you have sacrificed your own poetry for your scholarship – not to mention your classroom teaching? How do you strike a balance? And how has that balance shifted over the years?

Would that I could strike a balance. Unfortunately, in the choppy seas of conflicting claims, the best I can manage is to hang onto the tiller and hope not to get pitched from the deck. The worst period for the poetry was the mid to late 1990s, when I was putting together an edition of J.V. Cunningham's poems and trying to write *All the Fun's in How You Say a Thing*, in addition to dealing with a heavy teaching schedule.

Do you ever regret the time you spent on Missing Measures *and* All the Fun*?*

No. We have long needed to re-examine the standard views or explanations of modern poetry, which have remained for several generations now largely shaped by and weighted in favour of the theory of Ezra Pound and the practice of T. S. Eliot. Because the triumph of the experimentalists coincided with the establishment of the study of English literature as a university discipline, the normal process of sorting out over time – of letting the dust settle before attempting to determine what was and wasn't significant – didn't occur to the extent it had in earlier periods. Writers like Eliot and Joyce were more or less immediately canonized, and notions that were originally polemical – for instance, that modern verse had to be fragmentary and difficult in response to a chaotic and trying age – came to be adopted as descriptive truths. And many subsequent critics and poets have embraced and propounded the illogical principle that modern or contemporary poems that aren't experimental aren't modern or contemporary.

This is not to say that one outlook is wrong, and another is right. But the experimental movement left in its wake some narrow and proscriptive attitudes, and we'd all benefit if we could think more broadly and flexibly about Modernism and modern poetic practice.

What do you think is the most serious or disturbing effect of Modernism on verse technique?

The experimentalists identified metre with dated idiom. They felt that to get rid of stale diction and subject matter they had to get rid of traditional metre. I agree with Eliot and Pound that the bath water had to be thrown out; but the baby didn't need to go with it.

Technical matters aside, can you summarize your general feelings about Modernism?

We should prize its vitality, but be concerned about its tendency towards self-obsession and discontinuity. We perhaps have made too much of our singularity. Too often we've insisted that the present is radically different from the past, that the human is separate from the natural, that thought and feeling are opposed, and that subject and object are unconnected. We've dwelt so much on novelty and change that we've neglected and isolated ourselves from valuable resources and ideas from earlier periods; and we've very nearly deluded ourselves into believing that simple linearity is the only dimension of time and being. We exist of necessity on the surface of life, but under every instant lies a depth of experience vaster than we can imagine. And even when we feel that, as the Earl of Rochester puts it, 'The present moment's all my lot,' we also live backward by memory and forward by anticipation.

A characteristic irony of the twentieth century is that its most famous scientific revelation – Einstein's principle that temporal, spatial, and kinematic phenomena are related – was converted, in many circles, into a doctrine of subjectivism.

Can you elaborate a little on what you term the 'doctrine of subjectiv-

ism'?

Einstein observed, among other things, that the mass of an object is affected by its velocity. But many ignored that this and other 'relativistic' phenomena can be calculated by mathematics. They misinterpreted Einstein to mean that measurement is dependent on the preferences of the individual observer.

Incidentally, Einstein repeatedly inveighed against this misconstruction. And on various occasions he expressed dissatisfaction with the term 'Theory of Relativity', which Max Planck had originally applied to the Lorentz-Einstein equations for the motion of electrons. For Einstein, relativity – meaning 'relatedness' – was simply a principle to be considered in formulating a more general view of the physical universe. And he felt that Felix Klein's 'Theory of Invariants' more accurately described his ideas.

In any event, we'd do a better job of caring for each other, our fellow creatures, and our planet if we acknowledged and explored connections as much as we have divisions. It is interesting that Eliot – for all his earlier emphasis on fragmentation, dissociation, and dislocation – came around to something like this view in his later work. The interpenetration of past, present, and future is the great theme of *Four Quartets*.

As you indicate, you are hardly as unsympathetic to Pound and Eliot as your critics sometimes say you are.

In one respect, the leaders of the experimental movement were like characters in Greek tragedy, in that their innovations produced results exactly the opposite of those they intended. Free verse, for instance, was originated to make poetry more challenging. Would it be possible, without metre, to create poetry with the rhythmical coherence, force, and subtlety of traditional verse? This was, in the early years of the twentieth century, a fresh and bracing enterprise. Yet, in short order, free verse became an excuse for an anything-goes aesthetic. Moreover, many poets started using free verse as a means of avoiding the sustaining exigencies of poetic craft.

In Missing Measures, *you point out that when Pound, Eliot and William Carlos Williams recognized that this was happening, they were horrified.*

Yes, and by the century's end, free verse had eclipsed not only metrical poetry, but itself. To be genuinely free, free verse needs something to be free from, and the metrical tradition had been pretty much lost.

Which is why you wrote All the Fun's in How You Say a Thing *as well as* Missing Measures ...

After *Missing Measures* appeared, a friend commended me on explaining why so many modern poets had abandoned metre; but she added that this had created a literary environment in which few people understood traditional versification. Wasn't it now incumbent on me to explicate, in a contemporary and reader-friendly way, metre and its expressive resources? Though this question made me wince – I did not at the time want to undertake another prose project – I recognized that she had a point.

You might have winced for other reasons. Your scholarship also conflicts with your teaching – and teaching in turn must have deflected you from your poetry as much as the scholarship has.

The demands of teaching are steady and insistent. You want your classes to be organized, intellectually substantial, and lively. When essays come in, your must read them carefully and fairly, and return them promptly to the students. It's important to give extra time to students having special interests or needs. In contrast, the Muses don't materialize at your elbow at 8am five mornings a week with buckets of inspiration. They lurk thoughtfully and quietly in the background, and if you are to hear them, you must be quiet and attentive, too. You have to shelter time to focus inwardly. If you teach, there will be long stretches when you don't have the opportunity to do this. But this is true of almost any regular employment. Short of being independently wealthy, all poets have to labour at some trade or other to keep bread in the cupboard.

That's the down side of teaching. Does that daily labour recompense you in any way?

The myth of the ivory tower notwithstanding, you're never isolated as a teacher. Whether you're discussing *Daniel Deronda* with an upper-division seminar, or explaining to a first-year student the difference between the active and passive voices, you're reminded that everybody has intellectual ambitions and yearnings and that we should consecrate some of our energy to serving them as well as our own concerns.

Also, one of your responsibilities as a teacher is to help liberate students from the merely contemporary – to show them larger and richer possibilities of thought and experience. And you yourself may become clearer-headed and better-grounded as a result of being regularly obliged to re-read, re-think, and introduce to students to great works of literature.

Let's return to your scholarship for a moment: in your landmark Missing Measures, *you state your credo: 'I believe that our ability to organize thought and speech into measure is one of the most precious endowments of the human race.' That's quite a statement.*

Day-to-day life is often chaotic and brutally irrational, but I think most of us feel, whenever we contemplate the universe, that there's an order and beauty fundamental to it and to reality itself. Art and science alike, it seems to me, endeavor to understand that order and beauty – its nature and its laws. And one of the best ways we can ameliorate the human condition is by appreciating and affirming that order and beauty. In thoughtfully articulating our experience, poetry is one of those pursuits that enacts and strengthens what is best in reality and in us. It is verbal intelligence set into durable form.

Several of your poems seem explicitly religious, such as the 'Faith' section of 'Notes Toward Definition', 'A Devotional Sonnet' and 'Angel'. And you have poems about the Biblical figures Joseph and King David.

It is difficult for me to imagine that our universe, which is so elegant and so complex, could have evolved and could exist without a creative intelligence behind it. I also believe, with the writer or writers of Genesis, that the created world is good and that its historical horrors and depravities result chiefly from human greed and folly. And I have always been moved by the story of Jesus, and by the message of his ministry – that Divinity wishes us well and shares in our joys and suffering.

Your expression of the 'message of his ministry' sounds like rather liberal theology. Unitarian, perhaps?

When I was growing up Burlington, Vermont, my family attended the First Unitarian Church there. I know that Unitarians are considered to be thoroughly secular and to believe in only, to use the humorous formula, the Fatherhood of God and the Brotherhood of Man in the Neighbourhood of Boston. But in Sunday School, we read and studied the Bible, especially Genesis, the story of the Exodus, some of the Psalms, and the three Synoptic Gospels. John may have been considered a little too tendentious and doctrinal.

That's the theological side. What about practice? Did any experiences of the church particularly influence you?

The church held, each December, a Christmas pageant, which, though staged and enacted by the church and its members, was attended by many people in Burlington of all different faiths. The pageant told the story of the nativity by means of carols. There was a manger in the front of the church; as the carols progressed, more and more of the *dramatis personae* of the nativity entered from the rear of the church and took their places at or near the manger. The Holy Family appeared, then an angel announcing the Good News, then the shepherds, then the magi, and so forth.

The church is one of those austerely beautiful old Federal-style churches, and the pageant took place in the evening, with candles lit in the simple plain glass windows. Toward the end of the service, smaller candles passed to the congregation and were lighted. It was magical. We always looked forward to the pageant, and, for a time, from perhaps the ages of eight to twelve, I was the right height for supporting roles. One year I played a shepherd boy; another year I was an attending servant of the magi.

These early experiences in the church were, I suspect, almost as important as the instruction I received in elementary school, though I hasten to add that I'm grateful that my religious education and my public education were not mixed.

You refer, in your Frost essay, 'Across Spaces of the Footed Line', to your hope that the twenty-first century will 'heal the terrible breach between rhythm and metre that occurred in the 20th century'. Of course, few modern poets admit to being a-rhythmical: what are you observing in suggesting that they aren't?

I meant not that they're a-rhythmical, but that they're a-metrical. Most speech has some degree of rhythm. Metre organizes that rhythm. Frost himself has a nice comment about this: 'They use the word "rhythm" about a lot of free verse; and gee, what's the good of the rhythm unless it is on something that trips it – that it ruffles? You know, it's got to ruffle the metre. ... There's both the metre and the expressiveness on it – and so we get a poem.' What you have in much current verse is rhythm and expressiveness, but these elements are not playing on or against a metre. You don't have the fixed measure shaping the rhythm and enabling its modulations to be heard against a recurring, underlying pattern.

You've described that as 'Frost's love for the dialectic between prosodic rule and individual tonality'.

Yes, you have the fixed norm of metre interacting with the fluid and variable rhythms of actual speech.

Reading your essay on Frost, and comparing that to your other work in All's the Fun's in How You Say a Thing *and* Missing Measures, *I wonder to what extent you have based your own attitudes about metre on Frost's? As he described it, 'Poetry plays the rhythms of dramatic speech on the grid of metre.' Did Frost, who was a formative part of your childhood experience of poetry, as I recall, help form your own views? Or did you arrive at the same conclusions independently?*

Frost the theoretician was not an influence. His comments about versification are scattered here and there in his letters, his notebooks, the few essays he published in his lifetime, tapes of his readings, and transcripts of interviews with him. Only gradually did I realize that he was, in addition to being a wonderful poet, an extraordinarily insightful student of versification. I learned metre mostly by reading lots of poems. The two most helpful critical works I encountered as a student were Yvor Winters's excellent essay, 'The Audible Reading of Poetry', and James McAuley's fine handbook, *Versification: A Short Introduction.*

Frost was a powerful influence on your early years in Burlington, Vermont. Can you explain how that influence came about?

Frost lived for much of his adult life in Vermont, and became official state laureate toward the end of his life. Because of this, his poems were almost as much a part of my early education as *Charlotte's Web*, the Hardy Boys, Tom Swift, and *The Wind in the Willows*. I believe I first heard 'Stopping by Woods on a Snowy Evening' when my fourth- and fifth-grade teacher, Florence Keyes, read it one grey and snow-flurrying afternoon a day or two before Thanksgiving. It was in Grace McDonald's sixth-grade class, if memory serves, that we read several other Frost poems, including 'The Runaway'. This poem, which describes a Morgan colt frightened by a storm, made a vivid impression, since I had already read Marguerite Henry's classic *Justin Morgan Had a Horse* and I had visited, with my family or on a school field trip, the famous Morgan Horse Farm down near Middlebury.

And yet, you never met Frost.

When he passed on, I was still in junior high school – middle school, as it's now called. Though entranced by the descriptive beauties of Frost's poems, I had, at that age, only the haziest sense of authorship. The stories and poems we read seemed as much a part of our natural environment as the air around us. It took a while to realize that they were created by real people. I regret this now because Frost read his poems, once or twice in the late 1950s or early 1960s, at Ira Allen Chapel up the hill in Burlington at the University of Vermont – UVM as it's known locally and regionally. If I had known enough to ask, my parents would surely have taken me to hear him. On other occasions, roughly around that time or a little later, my parents took me to concerts there or elsewhere on the UVM campus by Pete Seeger and Harry Belafonte.

Did Burlington offer any formative cultural experiences you would like to share?

The university offered an annual programme of cultural events called the Lane Series – the 'Lane' part must have referred to a sponsor or donor. These performances were held down at the Memorial Auditorium on the corner of Main and Union Streets, and my parents took me to a number of them. One of these featured Andrés Segovia, who, despite being fairly far along in years, played with extraordinary energy and delicacy.

Later, on my own in high school, I attended at the Patrick Gym a memorable concert by Bob Dylan. He performed the first half alone; he came on with just his acoustic guitar. After a break, however, he reappeared with his back-up band, the Hawks, and the evening became electric, literally and metaphorically. Many of Dylan's folk-music fans got up in protest and walked out; they streamed away down the aisles.

The Hawks, I should add, were incredibly loud. They could rock 'n roll, but they were not yet the tight and accomplished ensemble that I saw perform at Tufts University some years later. By that time, they had changed their name to The Band and were well known in their own right.

I note a musical influence in your poetry – I'm thinking particularly of 'Education in Music' and 'The Treatise on Harmony', in which an orchestra tuning its instruments becomes a metaphor for the activities of children after school's out. The Hawks don't seem to have been a likely influence – what was? How do you see music as contributing to your poetry – and perhaps even to your decision to become a poet?

Music had no direct effect on that decision, though there is a musical influence, as you suggest, in some of my verse. Among classical composers, Haydn has always been a special favourite, and two of my poems – 'Last Tango' and the poem you mention, 'Education in Music' – draw on his music and life. Also, there was a time in the mid-1970s when I attended dress rehearsals of the San Francisco Symphony. You'd go down to the symphony hall on Wednesday morning at eight-thirty and, for several dollars, receive a cup of coffee, a doughnut, and a short lecture on the principal piece the orchestra was preparing that week. Then you'd sit in on the rehearsal. Seeing the musicians and conductor take apart and reassemble Beethoven's Sixth or a Mozart piano concerto may have eventually contributed to 'The Treatise on Harmony'.

Misleading analogies have been drawn between poetry and music, but they are sister arts. Both involve measure, and both develop arguments that appeal to the full sensibility and not simply the logical faculty. Further, many musical forms – from masses to operas to folk songs – involve words as well as notes. Even pop lyrics – which lean on their instrumental settings and tend toward stereotypical phrasings – have at their best the same verbal delight that characterizes good poetry. The scholar Blanford Parker once remarked that the lyrics of Paul McCartney's 'I've Just Seen a Face' are, in their play of sound and in their strophic structure, as ingenious as the stanzas of Herrick and Hardy.

In Burlington, there was a fairly significant Shakespeare festival, too – yes?

The University of Vermont had a wonderful summer Shakespeare festival. The festival's directors aimed to do (and ultimately succeeded in doing) all of the plays in the Shakespearean canon, three per summer. Beginning at the age of twelve or thirteen, and continuing through and beyond my high-school years, I regularly attended the plays, sometimes reading or re-reading the texts the day of the performance. So I ended up knowing most of Shakespeare's work by the time I was twenty.

What were the performances like?

They were generally excellent. The major roles were performed by professional New York City actors from Actors Equity; most of the supporting roles were given to students in the drama department at the university and to other more or less local talent. The plays took place on the UVM campus in the small, attractive Royal Tyler Theater. There were ten or twelve rows of seats, which wrapped around three sides of the theatre, and a low stage occupied the fourth, backmost side. Consequently, we were always close to the performers, who made good use of the proximity by addressing their soliloquies directly to us.

Any favourite plays?

The histories. My favourites were *1 Henry IV,* and *Richard II.* The first production of the latter that I saw featured a wonderfully suave Bolingbroke. In the days that followed, I imitated his slightly impatient, casually commanding air, and I swaggered around, as he had done, with my hands tucked behind me into my belt. Unfortunately, I had none of the physical requisites to sustain this impersonation, and I had to drop it after being repeatedly asked if I was feeling all right.

My liveliest memory of the festival involves the fifth act of a performance of *Richard III.* The actors made their entrances and exits not only from the back of the stage, but also from the two aisles that led from the lobby down into the theatre; and in the climactic scene, the monstrous king rushed in from the lobby and, glaring wildly around at the audience, demanded, 'A horse! A horse! My kingdom for a horse!' His eyes met mine – I was sitting in the second row that night – and, for a terrifying instant, it seemed that he held me personally responsible for his pedestrian condition. I would have screamed had he not, almost immediately, dashed up the other aisle and back out to the lobby. No one was more relieved than I when the Earl of Richmond appeared a moment later with the news that the bloody dog was dead.

You make Burlington sound like an out-of-the-way cultural hub.

It offered a lot to a young person. One other thing I can mention – not that it has anything directly to do with writing – is that every summer from 1956 to 1960, with the exception of 1958, the New York Giants, the professional football team, held their annual pre-season training camp at Saint Michael's College in Winooski, right across the river from Burlington. The practices were open to the public; my brother, sister, and I were great Giant fans; and it was wonderful to see our heroes at close range – Emlen Tennell, Jimmy Patton, Sam Huff, Andy Robustelli, Rosey Grier, Dick Lynch, Charley Conerly, Roosevelt Brown, Frank Gifford, Alex Webster, Mel Triplett, Kyle Rote, and on and on. Jim Lee Howell was the coach, and his assistants included Tom Landry and Vince Lombardi.

It's odd that many see you as a quintessentially California poet, with poems like 'Near Olympic' and 'Pacific Rim'. Yet California entered your life relatively late – you even talk about that psychological transition a bit in 'December in Los Angeles'. Why did the dye take so deeply?

It was a combination, or rather a succession, of things. In the summer of 1964, my mother took my brother, sister, and me on a cross-country trip to visit the national parks. We hauled a tent trailer behind our little Plymouth Valiant. When we arrived in California, I was much taken with its deserts, its dry gold hills and valleys with live oak trees, and its magnificent coast. Also, we stayed several days with family friends east of Los Angeles, in Glendora, which at that time still had citrus orchards; I remember driving around with the windows rolled down and breathing in the wonderful, thick heavy scent of orange blossoms.

Back in Vermont, we had a friend named Walter Bogart, who was a political scientist at Middlebury and who had taught at Stanford in the 1930s. When I started to think about attending college, he urged me to apply to Stanford. When they accepted me, and offered financial aid into the bargain, I jumped at the chance to go back to the West Coast. Then, in 1969, while I was an undergraduate, my mother remarried – she and my father had divorced in the early 1960s. Her new husband was a biochemist at UVM and had a grant to teach and do research at the University of Cali Medical School in Colombia. My mother and my stepfather Erland ended up spending most of the next decade in Cali. During that time, I didn't have the emotional connection with Vermont that I'd had before or that I developed or re-developed after my mother and stepfather retired and moved back to Westmore, in the so-called Northeast Kingdom of Vermont, near Lake Willoughby. Especially after I returned to California upon completing my doctoral course work at Brandeis, the Golden State felt more and more like home. My wife is a native Angelina, and our marriage in 1979 sort of completed the process of assimilation.

Colombia must have been an exotic break. It is supposed to be one of the most beautiful countries in the world.

Because I visited just twice – I spent the Christmas holidays there one year and the Easter holidays there another – I can speak in only the most superficial and touristic way about Colombia. But it is a beautiful and varied country. It also is – and was, though not the extent it became later – unsettled politically. A colleague once invited my stepfather to a tree farm, where trees were being raised for timber. Erland had been there once before, but couldn't for some reason this second time. So his friend went by himself and was kidnapped by FARC. They ended up holding him for several years before releasing him. And I remember being struck, during a visit to Popayán, a lovely town up in the Andes south of Cali, by the contrast between the almost paradisiacal setting of the place and the many soldiers patrolling it. The soldiers were all armed with automatic weapons, and most of them looked to be in their teens or barely out of them. That was sad and disturbing.

Overall, however, Mother and Erland found the experience of Colombia very life-enhancing. She started a successful cooperative for the women in a barrio near where they lived; they made macramé purses and related items and eventually found an American distributor for their products. And my stepfather enjoyed teaching at the university. Though there was a prolonged strike that closed the campus for some time, and though there was some anti-American sentiment, his students much liked and respected him personally. He died in 2003, but up to the end he remained – and my mother continues to remain – in contact with a number of their Colombian friends.

Your mother was a powerful early influence on your poetic imagination, I understand.

She was. She often read to my sister, my brother, and me. And she read, among other things, *Mother Goose*, *A Child's Garden of Verses*, Edward Lear's 'The Owl and the Pussycat', *The Cat in the Hat*, and Eugene Field's 'Wynkin, Blynkin, and Nod'.

Isn't that a fairly common doorway to poetry – nursery rhymes, children's poetry, which is mostly rhymed and metred, even when in a sprung-rhythm sort of way? Children delight in these patterns, even when – perhaps especially when – the content is pure nonsense.

Even when my mother read content-laden material, we responded chiefly to the sound. She and my father grew up during the Great Depression, and came through the Second World War; he served as a sergeant in the

Army in the 156th Field Artillery Battalion in Europe, and she was for a time a nurse in New York City. And she liked to read that passage from 'Locksley Hall' in which Tennyson expresses the hope we'll eventually achieve a peaceful and just internationalism under universal law. The political or ethical theme was beyond me, but the rhythm was so stirring that even today I have by heart the famous lines that begin, 'For I dipt into the future, far as human eye could see ...'

It's such a simple thing. What led people to believe adults would react any differently to poetry? That pretty much brings us directly back to Missing Measures.

It's baffling, isn't it, that so many poets regard metre as repressive rather than as imaginatively delightful and stimulating. Composers of popular music never made this mistake. Maybe we poets should take a hint from lyricists like Irving Berlin, Lorenz Hart, Carole King, the Beatles, Joni Mitchell, and Bruce Springsteen.

Despite these early influences, you initially decided to be a mathematician.

In school I enjoyed arithmetic and mathematics. Beginning in elementary school, I was placed in an experimental accelerated mathematics program. But, looking back, I was never deeply committed to the subject, nor did I have any great gift for it. Even now, the thing I remember best from calculus class is composing a variation on the witches' song in *Macbeth*, in hopes that the forces of darkness would help us with our grades. Our song ended,

> Eye of newt, and fin of shark,
> Make Mr Gleason raise my mark.

Was that your first poem, perhaps?

If I remember correctly, that was a collaborative effort with Jimmy Martin, a friend with whom I sometimes attended the Shakespeare plays and who was also in that Algebra class.

More seriously, what finally nudged you in the direction of literature?

I loved reading, and, when I arrived at Stanford, I had a fine Freshman

English teacher – she was a teaching assistant – named Anne Phillips. Also, on my first-term schedule was an exciting seminar – all freshmen at that time were assigned a special freshman seminar – in Literature and Theology, in which we read novels by Dostoevsky, Malraux, Silone, Camus, and others. This was taught by another fine graduate student named Eugene England. Though I didn't declare a major in English until my junior year, these early teachers and classes tilted me to literature, as did, subsequently, such other outstanding teachers of literature as Nancy Packer, Kenneth Fields, Albert Guerard, Claude Simpson, Martin Evans, and Ian Watt.

Was Yvor Winters teaching at Stanford then?

He had retired and was very ill with the cancer that would kill him. But he had left a strong legacy. Many of the graduate students and younger faculty read and studied poetry with an enthusiasm and keenness that you rarely find today, alas, in the academy. Added to this, the Stanford campus was close to San Francisco and Berkeley, themselves intensely literary communities. The Beat Movement was still relatively recent and fresh. It was probably only natural that a bookish student would, coming to the university at that time, be drawn to the study of literature.

And yet, there's a link between mathematics and metre. That's part of the fun, isn't it? It appeals to the mathematical part of the brain as well. Perhaps that's one reason why Joseph Brodsky called poetry an accelerated mental process.

Brodsky's way of putting it is very apt. In different and illuminating ways, Frederick Turner and the late Henri Coulette have noted that metre appeals to both the left brain and the right. It engages both our semantic-logical capacities and our musical-intuitional ones. It allows us to experience language more richly than any other literary medium does.

It still wasn't clear you would throw your lot with poetry when you were a graduate student, was it? You did your dissertation on the history and conventions of detective fiction.

I relished Renaissance literature and twentieth-century literature, but felt weak in the nineteenth century. Heaven knows it's impossible to 'master' nineteenth-century literature: there are simply too many mega-novels and mega-novelists. But writing on the detective story obliged me to read and think about nineteenth-century fiction writers, such as Balzac, Poe, Dickens, Hugo, Trollope, Collins, and Doyle. Another concern – you touched on this earlier – was that I didn't want to get overly involved in the analysis of poetry when I myself was beginning to write it. Finally, I had always enjoyed reading mysteries – first, the Hardy Boys, and later, Rex Stout, Agatha Christie, Dashiell Hammett, and Raymond Chandler.

J.V. Cunningham supervised that dissertation. It wasn't quite his subject, was it?

Jim was interested in many things, including detective stories. Indeed, his first collection has a nice epigram, 'With a Detective Story', about mysteries. And as that poem suggests, he was intrigued by the ways in which the detective story embodies the Aristotelian plot – the carefully concatenated narrative that aims at producing surprising reversals and recognitions, without violating plausibility.

What, in particular, interested you about the detective stories?

For one thing, its conflicted attitude towards science. Detective fiction reflects both a faith in and a scepticism about science. The great hope of mystery stories is that if we just get our facts right, everything will be solved; and the great anxiety is that, even if we get our facts right, tragedy will still occur. As shrewd as Inspector Bucket is, he's always one step too late. This happens even to Sherlock Holmes sometimes. And as pure a rationalist and materialist as Javert is, he is betrayed and destroyed by a single inexplicable and irrational impulse.

Another interesting thing about detective fiction is that though it involves a belief in law, the detective – especially the private detective – is often aware of the shortcomings of a strictly legal justice; and he or she often is obliged to resolve conflicts between equity and law.

Also appealing is the way that detective stories suggest that we're all related. In *Bleak House*, a vast gulf evidently separates Lady Dedlock from Esther and from poor Jo the crossing-sweeper; but Dickens shows us this is an illusion. This same sense of everyone's being inter-connected informs the hard-boiled novels that Chandler and Ross MacDonald wrote about Southern California; and, to switch media, it informs John Sayles's terrific movie mystery, *Lone Star*.

You once said that Cunningham supported your poetry 'with his characteristic and supportive brevity'. Could you be a little less brief yourself?

How did he support you?

His interest by itself was cheering. He was not merely accomplished as a writer, but formidable as an individual. He was especially imposing in the classroom – tall and lean, with a penetrating gaze and a low, deliberate voice. We students were in awe of him, and he scared some of his colleagues to death. To hear him say, as he did on several occasions when I was starting to write, 'This is a real poem,' was manna from heaven, or at least from Parnassus. You could live on it for a long time.

Some have said that his severity was part of a persona he created.

When he was younger, he developed that tough exterior as a means of shielding himself from the world. He suffered terribly during the Depression. For a time in his late teens he wandered homelessly throughout the Southwest, trying to eke out a living with odd jobs and writing for the trade journals – the business magazines – of that era. In later years, he regretted his severity. He said in conversation that it was not good to have an image that you felt obliged to live up to; and even though he was aware of his image, I'm not sure he was aware of just how much it sometimes intimidated others. Once a fellow graduate had expressed astonishment that I spoke casually with him from time to time. This student regarded him as utterly unapproachable. I never told Jim this story; it would have pained him. He had a deep and catholic respect for others and otherness, and, for all his concentrated integrity, he was the last person in the world to be intentionally overbearing.

Cunningham exemplifies what Cicero called 'the plain style' – lean, spare, finely crafted, sparing of showy metaphor and gewgaws. You, too, have often been put in that basket.

I greatly admire the intellectual power and focus of Jim's poems, such as 'Poets survive in fame' and 'Meditation on Statistical Method'; and I tried, when I was starting out, to imitate his epigrams and to learn from, as he had, the fine epigrammatic poets of Latin and English – Catullus and Martial, Ben Jonson, Herrick, and Landor. But personal taste and temperament inclined me more to poetry like Sidney's, Keats's, or Hardy's. It's difficult to characterize one's own verse, but I'm probably more interested in imagery and metaphor than Jim was. And I perhaps write in – for whatever these categories are worth – the middle style more often than the plain.

I was aware of the 'plain' and 'high' styles – but I guess I could use a little brushing up on the 'middle' style.

In Cicero's analysis, the three styles – the plain, the middle, and the high – all aim in their ways for three virtues: correctness, clarity, appropriateness. The plain (or acute) style differs from the other two – the middle (or pleasant) and the high (or grand) – in that it eschews a fourth quality that the other styles seek. This is 'ornamentation', which includes figures of speech, richness and variety of language, and so forth. The middle style tends to receive short shrift in rhetorical discussions, because these concern first and foremost the training of orators aiming for legal or political careers. The plain style will obviously be useful to an orator engaged in the demonstration of fact and the high style will obviously be useful for orator who wishes to move the emotions of a magistrate or jury. The middle style, which aims at being attractive and which is particularly associated with the appealing use of metaphor and other figures, is more likely to appear in philosophical and poetical writing than in legal and political oratory.

But, as Cicero says, no writer uses one style exclusively, and the ideal poet or orator is the one who, like Homer or Demosthenes, is able to move fluidly between all levels of style. And as Quintilian says, there are infinite graduations of style and many possible blendings of them. Even Cunningham, who pretty purely embodies the plain style, uses the other styles on occasion. Especially in his earlier poems, such as 'The Phoenix' and 'The Wandering Scholars', he has moments of rhetorical violence as startling as those in John Donne, Hart Crane, or Allen Tate.

What do you think critics are pinpointing when they call you a 'plain stylist', then?

Possibly my association with Cunningham, and possibly they are noting that my work seems clear, compared to the obscurity that you find in so much contemporary poetry. It's for this same reason that Frost, Bogan, Auden, Wilbur, and Larkin have sometimes been referred to as plain stylists. Because they speak comprehensibly, are grammatically correct, focus their tropes, and employ language suited to their subject matter, they seem 'plain'. But they're working on – or moving between – different levels of style, and are not predominantly plain in the sense that Cunningham is.

You and I both know that many readers will find these distinctions pe-

dantic and factitious. Can you defend them? How do you see them as useful in discussing contemporary verse?

I wouldn't want to force these distinctions on anyone, and I'm not sure how useful they are today. I'm not suggesting that a glorious poetic renaissance would occur if we would only take up and con our trusty volumes of Cicero, Quintilian, and the Senecas. Yet, as Paul Valéry remarks somewhere, the ancient study of rhetoric, however peculiar in many respects, gave people a means of discussing style and, even more important, taste.

Taste is a subject that isn't often connected with verse – especially not contemporary verse.

Taste is as critical to poetry as metrics and versification, but hardly anybody talks about taste nowadays. This is one reason that so much contemporary verse is banal and crude. We think, rightly, we should be allowed to address any subject, but we also think, wrongly, that we can just barge ahead with our liberty. Hence we often read – or hear at poetry readings – poems in which poets describe, with unhappily misplaced specificity, their sex life or family history. Touchy subjects can be made poetical, but one needs literary tact to treat them. This tact can be learned by reading and absorbing the examples of good models; but the study of rhetoric can also help create the necessary sensitivity.

Cunningham's wife, Jessie MacGregor Campbell, was an Austen scholar. I note that Austen is one of the subjects you teach – is there a connection?

No, though we talked of Austen over the years. I started teaching Austen simply because she was one of those major authors – Milton is another – who seemed to be increasingly slighted in the curricular stampedes to modern, contemporary, and American literature. Perhaps with the success of the recent movies based on her novels and the excellent BBC serialization of *Pride and Prejudice*, she'll return to her rightful and prominent position on school syllabi. Students love her. Once they start reading her aloud and hearing the rhythms of her prose, they really tune into her humour. And her prime subject is the dysfunctional family, which is about as close to a universal subject as there is. Pretty much everybody can, as they say, relate to it.

We've talked a great deal about novels so far. You've mentioned to me before your interest in the relationship of poems and novels – even poems as mini-novels.

Like many readers, I love the circumstantiality of a good novel – the way you can sink into it and live for a time among its characters. And several of my early poems examine ideas or situations suggested by novels. 'Life Portrait', for example, is a meditation on the relationship, in *David Copperfield*, between the hero and Dora Spenlow; it explores, in connection with that relationship, our tendency not to prize things until we've lost them.

More recent poems, including 'In the Italian Alps' and 'The Middle Years', attempt to create a sense of character and situation, such as you find in a novel. I don't know how successful these are. But I am interested in trying, without becoming long-winded or Browningesque, to incorporate into some of my poems elements of prose fiction.

You've spoken about Henry James and Ivan Turgenev being influences on you. Could you describe that influence a little?

They both are able, without being preachy or didactic, to communicate a profoundly moral sense of experience. James's *Wings of the Dove* is like an extended and beautiful symbolist poem. Its coordinates – its scenes and actions – are its meaning. No Greek tragedy concludes with a greater sense of catastrophe, but James works out the plot so well that he doesn't need to say anything overtly. You yourself feel, you know in your nerves, how much Densher has been touched by the wings of the dove – by Milly – and you feel as keenly as he does how nothing now can redeem his relationship with Kate.

You get similar feelings from the shorter works of Turgenev and James. In Turgenev's 'First Love' or James's 'Madame de Maeves' – to take two examples – you have that same brave illumination of a situation, yet there's no intrusive analysis or authorial manipulation of sentiment. Everything's in the presentation.

That is what many of us as poets want to do, at least some of the time. We hope to reveal and express human realities, but to do so in a way that is immediate and all the more powerful for not resorting to explicit commentary.

James and Turgenev are also, with Chekhov, perhaps the pre-eminent masters of that delectable form, the novella. In James generally, there is the problem of his increasingly elaborate style; and, as much as I like *The*

Ambassadors and *The Wings of the Dove*, I prefer the early and middle novels and stories. And at times James is so much a student of sensibility – is so immersed in impressions he creates – that you're not sure he's got a grip on their significance. Are the ghosts in 'The Turn of the Screw' real? Or is that tale a study, as Edmund Wilson and other have argued, of suppressed hysteria? It's hard to say – and it's not one of those works where we can have it both ways, because the two interpretations lead us to such very different assessments of or feelings about the governess.

But, taken all in all, James is wonderful writer, and a wonderfully consistent one. Though prolific, he managed to write at a high level almost all the time.

How much free verse have you written over the years? 'Nightpiece' comes to mind. So does 'But Home is Here' – although it seems very loosely accentual. Correct me if I'm wrong.

No, you're correct. 'Snapshots for Posterity' is another. I was – and remain – interested in vers libre. If I've favored metre, it's not that I don't admire good free verse. It's just that you can do much more with metre. When you have the bass of the metrical line, you can modulate and focus language more subtly and memorably.

What motivated you to write your first poems? How old were you?

I very occasionally tried to write verse when I was attending the public /state schools in Burlington, but I didn't seriously start writing poems until the middle or latter stages of my undergraduate education. I believe that the main reason I started was that I loved poems and wanted to see if I could make them myself. I also wanted, though this desire was felt at first only obscurely, to preserve things. It bewildered and saddened me that all the marvels and miracles of life were transient. Everything passes. Though poetry, too, will pass, it arrests the process for a while and perhaps points to something that does not pass.

I suppose that theme underlies all good poetry, really – from Homer to Shakespeare's Sonnets *to T.S. Eliot's* Four Quartets. *But how, in particular, do you see it reflected in yours?*

Recently, looking through the poems, with a view to selecting a group to present at a reading, I noticed that many concern fragility. 'At Will Rogers Beach', for instance, is concerned with the fragility of the natural world,

'The Library' with the fragility of culture and learning, and 'Her Memory of the Picnic' with the fragility of relationships. By the same token, a number of other poems, such as 'Portrait of the Artist as a Young Child' and 'Toward the Winter Solstice', attempt to discover or to be open to an experience of transcendence.

You turned to more structured verse quite young, didn't you? When was that?

When I started writing poetry, my admiration for Frost made me cautious about proceeding before learning metrical technique. Going forward without knowing the time-tested rules would have made me feel like someone who aspired to write piano concertos without learning scales. Then, too, most of the poems I best remembered were in metre. I realized that if my poems were to give others the pleasure that the poems I loved had given me, I'd need to learn to write in metre.

Others clearly don't feel the same.

No, and that's fine, though more young poets would explore metre if they were exposed to it and if there were not so much hostile propaganda against it. In the winter of 1987, UCLA's Extension School asked me to teach a class in metrical composition, and several excellent *vers libristes* enrolled. At the end of class, they approached me and said that, now that they understood metre, they preferred it. They even asked me if they should burn their earlier free-verse poems! I laughed and told them, no, they should keep them; the modes didn't have to be mutually exclusive. But once people understand metre, most of them recognize that it's not just a restriction, but is also a liberating source of symmetries and surprises.

And fun. The pressure of, say, rhyme, metre, makes you find connections you didn't know you had in your head. There's an element of surprise with formally structured poetry, isn't there? That reaction: 'I didn't know I thought that!'

Joe Kennedy says that rhymes and related devices can be valuable disturbers of our unconscious mind and can allow us, when we're writing, to tap into and draw on our unconsciousness.

It can be dangerous, no doubt – Auden describes the temptation to dis-

honesty, saying something because it 'works' rather than because it is true.

Auden, I believe, was mostly talking about the temptation to say something for oratorical flourish, though of course an inexperienced poet may, as you observe, be tempted to write something simply because it meets the demands of metre or rhyme. When Auden famously denounced his ending of 'Spain'– 'History to the defeated / May say Alas but cannot help nor pardon' – he damned the lines not for being 'rhetorically effective', but for propounding the 'inexcusable' doctrine that success equals goodness. Since the poem is composed mostly in an unrhymed and loosely accentual measure, the form didn't force those words on him.

Actually, I was thinking of a perhaps more famous example. Auden banned 'September 1, 1939', from his postwar Collected because of the line 'We must love one another or die':

> And the lie of Authority
> Whose buildings grope the sky:
> There is no such thing as the State
> And no one exists alone;
> Hunger allows no choice
> To the citizen or the police;
> We must love one another or die.

Certainly the neat anapestic trimeter of the line, plus the rhymes with 'lie' and 'sky' give a sense of ringing inevitability to what came to be the hated line for Auden. Rereading it after its publication, he wrote that he said to himself: '"That's a damned lie! We must die anyway." So, in the next edition, I altered it to "We must love one another and die." This didn't seem to do either, so I cut the stanza. Still no good. The whole poem, I realized, was infected with an incurable dishonesty and must be scrapped.' Well, history hasn't agreed with his interpretation of the line, in the poem that Auden called 'trash which [he was] ashamed to have written'.

I see what you're driving at. Certainly even our best poets can be tempted to say things for rhetorical or rhythmical effect that they don't believe or haven't sufficiently examined. All poets must be on guard against that.

John Fuller's excellent commentary on Auden has a thorough discussion of Auden's mixed and shifting feelings about 'September 1, 1939'. Concerning the love-or-die line in particular, Auden may have been too hard on himself and too literal-minded. When he refers to our dying, I think principally not of physical extinction, but of the spiritual death we suffer when we fail to acknowledge our relations to the larger human community and our responsibilities to others.

Auden's revisions are an incredibly tangled issue. They range from sensibly straightforward excisions of unnecessary obscurities – such as those of the Captain Ferguson part of 'Taller Today' – to the radical and controversial deletions or retrenchments we've mentioned. Another instance in this latter category is the dropping of the stanza about Kipling and Paul Claudel from 'In Memory of W. B. Yeats'. I seem to remember that in that case Auden felt he had been unfair to Kipling. Just as Byron came to feel that he'd been unjust to Walter Scott and others in his 'English Bards and Scotch Reviewers', Auden came to believe that he'd advanced an over-simplified view of Kipling.

In your essay on Frost, you praise his loose iambics, astrophic iambics, etc. Yet you, personally, have pretty much abjured them in your own writing. Why?

Frost says that 'there are virtually but two [metres in English], strict iambic and loose iambic.' By 'loose iambic' he means iambic verse mixed or varied with occasional anapests. I have a few pieces in loose iambics – for instance, 'Waiting for the Storm' from *Sapphics Against Anger and Other Poems*, and 'Advice to a Student' from *The Color Wheel*. But these are, as you suggest, exceptions. I'm not sure why this is. Maybe my preference began as partly a response to the times. When I started out, very few poets in my generation were working in metre: I may have figured that if I was going to write metrically, I might as well go all the way and see what I could do within the basic traditional lines.

You certainly draw on a glorious list of antecedents.

Well, of course, a lot of the great poetry in English is strict iambic – iambic verse, that is, in which the syllable count as well as the beat count is maintained consistently. This includes the frequently anthologized sonnets of Sidney, Shakespeare, Keats, Christina Rossetti, and Countee Cullen. It also includes the satirical verse of Dryden and Pope, *Paradise Lost,* Keats's odes, much of Frost and Bogan, Auden's social-commentary poems like 'On the Circuit' and 'Under Which Lyre', and Cunningham's epigrams. And it includes much of the great metred poetry of the generation before mine, including the poems of Wilbur, Larkin, Bowers, Hecht,

Pinkerton, Kennedy, Snodgrass, and Gunn.

Don't neglect E.A. Robinson! I understand you consider him a critical influence on your own work.

Yes. Robinson cautions us against common assumptions about verse forms. If we didn't have the text of 'Eros Turannos' before us, few of us would imagine that the stanza in which the poem is written – with its regular trot of tetrameters and trimeters and its jingly feminine rhymes – could produce anything more than *vers de société*. Yet the poem is a powerful, sophisticated, and compassionate analysis of human and sexual relations gone wrong. When you read Robinson, you realize that virtually any metrical or stanzaic structure – no matter how seemingly limited or antiquated – can be made fresh if you bring to it solid material and sincerity and skill.

Robinson doesn't have the lively idiomatic fluency of Frost, or the flash and fun of the early Stevens; but in his noble stoicism, he is as great as they are. Despite the apparent grimness of his subjects, his verse struggles to stay hopeful and humorous, and clings to faith and truth in the face of mortality and defeated hopes. One of my favourite passages in American poetry occurs in 'Isaac and Archibald', when the elderly Archibald says to the young protagonist:

> The shadow calls us, and it frightens us –
> We think; but there's a light behind the stars ...
> Live to see clearly and the light will come
> To you, and as you need it.

This, from a man who suffered as Robinson did, who came from that tragically broken family and who lived for much of his adult life in terrible poverty.

I quote from my recent interview with the North Dakota poet Tim Murphy: 'I made a compact with the devil when I started writing in trimeter and dimeter in the 1980s, and I said I can use any damn off-rhyme I choose, because I'm making my rhymes come every four syllables, or six syllables. Then when I read Tim Steele, I said, "This is preposterous, Murphy. You cannot be so sloppy. You have to live up to the example of the elder Tim."' Yet you haven't entirely abjured assonantal or slant rhymes, have you? I note rhymes like 'wealth' and 'twelfth' in 'Cory in April' and the even farther-flung 'innocence' and 'scenes' in 'With a Copy of Ronald

Firbank', although these clearly are exceptions to a larger pattern of true rhymes.

I wish I could say that I introduced the variant rhymes in those early poems in a cleverly calculated fashion that contributed to wonderfully subtle effects, but this wasn't the case. I was flying by the seat of my pants and crashing from time to time. But, as Tim indicates, from the beginning I've mostly used full or exact rhyme. And it's been quite a while since I've introduced off rhyme into my poems in the casual, occasional manner of those relatively early poems that you mention. These days when I use off rhyme, as in 'Homage to a Carnegie Library', or rich rhyme, as in 'For My Sister', I use it regularly throughout the poem. This, I hope, allows the reader to recognize the device as part of the poem's general structure. It also, I hope, serves to honour variant rhyme by developing it consistently and on its own terms.

You point out that Frost thinks of rhyme as the acoustic equivalent of metaphor – 'the extension of metaphor into sound'. It goes a bit beyond that, doesn't it? Dick Davis called it the mating of unlike things – like sex. I think Brodsky said pretty much the same – part of that accelerated mental process: 'Once you hook up one word, one concept to another, through a rhyme, once you've uncovered that these two things are connected, you get addicted to that linkage, to that ability to create that linkage, to not only the facility of the linkage but the certainty of that linkage. That's what you do on paper; you uncover the dependencies, the relationships which are built into the language. The general manner in which your mind starts to operate is coupling, coupling, coupling.'

Rhyme is magical not only because it matches sounds, but also, as Davis and Brodsky suggest, because it matches different ideas, different parts of speech, different images. Rhymes, at their most enchanting, are verbal aerialists, swinging high in the big top – flinging out to each other in mid-air to meet and catch together.

You have said, 'There are no rhymes that cannot be redeemed by the appropriate context.' Since the idea that you can't use certain rhymes amounts virtually to a superstition nowadays – I've heard people like Ken Fields and X.J. Kennedy voice some of this thinking – could you elucidate this matter?

As Alfred Corn says well in The Poem's Heartbeat, current taste opposes licenses available to earlier poets. Metrical poets especially are no longer supposed to use, for example, inversions of normal word order or archaisms. (Curiously, free verse poets still can and sometimes do get away with these devices, which appear to be less noticeable when rhythmical organization has been relaxed.) Contemporary metrical poets must also be cautious with schemes of sound like consonance, assonance, and alliteration. And the commoner rhymes, such as breeze/trees and breath/death, are deemed off limits.

I sympathize with this view, but I wouldn't want to make a rule of it. Any rhyme can be effective, given the right context. For instance, Larkin employs, in 'The Old Fools', that duo beloved of music-hall crooners – 'remember/September' – and it works fine. Here perhaps it is the context that saves the rhyme: Larkin is referring to bygone days when the old fools were bright young things.

It does seem that our taste in poetry is as subject to fashion as the Milanese runways or catwalks. For example, it's commonly said, almost a cliché, that English is a 'rhymed out' language. You don't agree?

Rhymes are not like fossil fuel. You don't pump them into poems and burn them up forever. They're recycleable and can, if used imaginatively, produce very different effects in different contexts.

There's a related point. Because words in English end so many different ways, it isn't a language with a wealth of multiple rhymes; and in this respect it is, as people have said, impoverished compared to, for instance, Italian and French. However, English is fabulously rich in rhyme pairs. Furthermore, new words are coming into the language every day. For instance, glancing through the opening pages of Vikram Seth's *Golden Gate*, I find pairs like 'flights/megabytes', 'Pink Floyd/annoyed', 'pride/formaldehyde', and 'Weetebix/26' – all fluidly integrated in the texture of the poem. Did anyone use these rhymes before Vikram? Not that this is the chief – or even one of the principal – merits of his or any poem. Rhyme, at its best, guides and points meaning. No poet who gracefully blends familiar and less familiar pairs will lack an audience.

X. J. Kennedy characterized your verse in these words: '[W]ithout surpassing his mentor Cunningham in concision or intensity, [he is] going considerably beyond him in depth and range.' He says you've got better since he wrote these words, over a decade ago. That's an important tribute.

Joe's been a great friend through thick and thin. It would be impossible to exaggerate how much his encouragement and good opinion have meant over the years.

How did your friendship come about?

I had admired Joe's poetry since undergraduate days when I'd come across and purchased, in a poetry bookshop, a copy of *Nude Descending a Staircase*. We started corresponding, in the early 1970s, when I was a graduate student at Brandeis, and when he and his wife Dorothy printed some of my work in their short-lived but important journal of metred verse, *Counter/Measures*. Beginning in the mid-1970s, he started re-printing a poem or two of mine in editions of his textbook *Introduction to Poetry*. For some years, this was, as far as I'm aware, almost the only place I was anthologized. But it was not until 1983, if I remember correctly, that we actually met.

Why do you consider his short-lived journal to have been important?

The contributors not only included great metrists of Joe's generation, such as Wilbur and Hecht; it also featured work by younger and then unknown writers interested in metre, like Charles Martin and Gjertrud Schnackenberg. *Counter/Measures* also ran reviews of worthy books overlooked by more mainstream publications. For instance, Dorothy wrote a notice of a collection of poems by Myra Cohn Livingston, a fine writer of children's verse whose work I had not previously known. Some years later, I moved to Los Angeles, where Myra lived. My wife and I eventually became friends with her; and we once dined at her house with Joe and his son Dave, who were visiting at the time.

It was a wonderful little magazine, though 'little' may be the wrong word. The issues appeared once a year and were quite plump.

I heard somewhere that you offered to revive Counter/Measures *after it had ceased publication.*

It was rash of me to propose that; and Joe, who was in England at the time, wrote a cautioning letter, for which I'm very grateful. He pointed out the energy and expense that the enterprise would involve, and suggested that I would be better off concentrating on my own work. I had no money and knew nothing of the logistics entailed in producing a journal. And though it would have been nice to have kept *Counter/Measures* going, Ben Jonson tells us that 'in short measures, life may perfect be.' However brief its run, the magazine had great verve and provided a lively forum for metrists and rhymers when few other journals were printing formal verse.

Some have termed the group of people who constellated around Yvor Winters and J.V. Cunningham, and the students of their students, the 'Stanford School of Poets'. That group would include, among others, Winters's wife Janet Lewis, Thom Gunn, Helen Pinkerton, Edgar Bowers, N. Scott Momaday, and by extension, Dick Davis, Rob Wells, and Clive Wilmer in the UK. While you were never a Winters student, certainly you are part of this grouping. Dana Gioia, in the 1970s, wrote: 'The Stanford style stresses the rational content of verse. Poetry must convey moral wisdom, Winters taught, through the disciplined and rational use of language. In his own mature work Winters also set the example of using metrical forms with strict regularity.' Well, that's one characterization.

If one thing unites the people you mention, it's their belief in intelligence – their belief that intelligence is valuable and that poetry profits from its exercise. But it is unfair, as I'm sure Dana would agree, to lump all of Winters's students together in one big, tough, moral/metrical mass. The best are all stylistically distinct from one another. If poetry had not drifted, in the second half of the twentieth century, so far into various irrationalities, the differences among Winters's associates would seem as obvious or more obvious than their similarities.

So you think any characterization of this group – whether as 'the Winters Circle' or the 'Stanford School' – is wholly illegitimate?

It's not primarily a question of legitimacy, but of usefulness and fairness. If a critic wishes to use those terms for taxonomic purposes, or to describe a general interest in coordinating thought and emotion, or simply to indicate friendly relations, near or distant, among a group of poets, that's fine. But many critics have used Winters as a brush to tar poets who hold views in any way resembling his, or who were or can be in any way associated with him. A jillion other influences, experiences, or ideas may have shaped the poets, and they may diverge from Winters on key points of style and outlook. But the critic need merely say, 'So-and-so are disciples of Winters' or 'She's just one of those Stanford poets,' and discussion ends. The putative disciples are convicted without trial of slavishly embracing all of Winters's views and are struck from the literary register, never having been engaged on their own terms. This happened repeatedly to Cunningham, and it's happened to some of the other poets you mentioned a moment ago.

The legacy of Yvor Winters is certainly controversial. Why the hostility to him? And why is so much of it so personal?

Partly because – to his great credit – he spoke so trenchantly and passionately about literature. And partly because – and this is less to his credit – he frequently did so in a manner that was abrupt or rebarbative.

That sounds like one of the more temperate opinions I've heard on the subject.

Winters was a great critic, who made many just and insightful comments about poets and poetry; but he didn't always present his positions as attractively, or develop them as flexibly, as he might have. Literary criticism is not an exact science. Its judgments are always to a degree provisional, and its opinions are effective thanks to their persuasive appeal as well as their logical force. It's a thin line between intellectual honesty and intellectual arrogance, and on occasion Winters crossed it.

Could you, in a few words, assess the historical role he played in American poetry and literature?

One role was mentioned by David Levin some years back in the *New York Review of Books*. Winters was instrumental in establishing American literature in the university curriculum. Others of his generation, of course, also contributed to this development; but his early critical books made a strong and thoughtful case for writers such as Melville, Dickinson, James, Wharton, Stevens, and William Carlos Williams. In this connection, Winters has suffered a particularly grave injustice. Later critics have damned him for qualifying his praise of people like Stevens and Williams, when those later critics might not have even been aware of these poets if Winters had not so perceptively and presciently championed them when they were little known.

Winters also had that important gift, which Pound had as well, for appreciating and calling attention to fine but neglected poets and poems. It is largely due to Winters that George Gascoigne, for instance, and Frederick Goddard Tuckerman – and Campion's 'Now winter nights enlarge' and George Herbert's 'Church Monuments' – are now available to be enjoyed in many current anthologies.

Winters's most durable contribution is his poetry. The best of his poems, such as 'A Summer Commentary', 'The California Oaks', 'Prayer for My Son', 'The Slow Pacific Swell', 'At the San Francisco Airport', are solidly and beautifully written.

I suppose the influence of Stanford writing, however we want to characterize it, has been extended to a new generation of poets, and not all of them at Stanford. You've been credited as an inspirational teacher and mentor – Vikram Seth, Leslie Monsour, and Kevin Durkin are among your protégés. What's the trick?

Each of those three poets is, of course, very gifted in his or her own way. If there is or was a trick to helping them, it was probably just to be attentive to, and encouraging of, their efforts. Since talent comes in so many different varieties and manifestations, formulas are of little use in assisting its development. A capacity for concern and appreciation is probably the most important aid.

I assume that you teach metre in your classes.

Yes, when the class involves poetry, whether it's a literature class or a writing class. We review metre, do scansion exercises, and read lots of poetry aloud. Though I encourage students to memorize poems they particularly like, I don't force them to memorize. Frost was probably right to say that it's not good to make people stick to poems unless the poems stick to them. If they don't really like something, and want to take it into heart and mind, memorization and recitation can become merely rote exercises, and no more conducive to the serious appreciation of literature than spelling bees are. Most students who grow to love poetry do memorize, with little or no prompting, at least a few of their favourite poems.

Creative writing programs have come under a great deal of attack lately – a logical swing of the pendulum in view of their proliferation in the 1970s. I know you occasionally teach creative writing courses – though most of your teaching is literature, particularly classical and medieval literature. What is your opinion of the creative writing industry and creative writing classes?

Because creative writing programs have been so roundly abused by so many people – including, strangely, those who run them – one almost feels obliged to say something in their favour. And, to be sure, taking a creative writing class or two can valuably inform students about literary technique and convention, and can give them a forum in which their writing may be shared and heard. Nevertheless, if we wish to support young writers, the first thing we should do is to encourage them to study as broadly as they can in the humanities and sciences. It is particularly misguided to encourage undergraduates to major in creative writing – and to examine in workshops, semester after semester, each other's apprentice efforts – when they would be better served by and would learn more from reading such authors as Shakespeare, Milton, Pope, Austen, Keats, Dickinson, George Eliot, Ibsen, James, Wharton, Tennessee Williams, and Ellison.

As regards MFA programs specifically, it has long been apparent that their proliferation has resulted in the artificial support and (ultimately cruel) encouragement of a large and ever-growing population of would-be writers – and would-be creative-writing teachers – who would be better off pursuing other goals and cultivating other talents. Moreover, just as the triumph of experimentalism coincided, in the early decades of the twentieth century, with the development of English Studies, so the writing program boom dovetailed, in the 1960s and 1970s, with the super-high tide of free verse; and consequently the numerous poets and poetry-writing teachers that the programs produced were almost entirely devoted to free verse. So the MFA programs played a key role in delivering the second blow of a double whammy – the first blow having been delivered by the original Modernists – against metre.

Finally, there is something troubling, conceptually, about creative writing. It suggests that other kinds of writing are non-creative or less organically vital. But in truth it probably takes as much skill, and maybe as much imagination, to write a great essay or a great work of history, biography, or science as it takes to write a fine poem or novel.

Poetry guides and handbooks have poured out of the presses like hot lava in recent years. How would you position All the Fun's in How You Say a Thing *among the others?*

I can't pretend to assess the book objectively vis-à-vis others in its field. I can tell you that I wanted to give a full – and, at the same time, user-friendly – treatment of versification. I aimed to be as comprehensive as possible, while at the same time maintaining readability.

Well, a review in the TLS *thought you succeeded, characterizing the book as 'elegantly written ... as entertaining and readable as it is erudite and taxonomically precise.'*

Before I started, there were useful handbooks on the market – perhaps most notably McAuley's *Versification: A Short Introduction* and John Hollander's *Rhyme's Reason*. There were as well excellent works, such as Derek Attridge's, that integrated elements of contemporary linguistics into the study of the versification. Older books by Edwin Guest, George Saintsbury, and Robert Bridges had retained – and still retain – their value. But there seemed to be a place for a detailed discussion of traditional accentual-syllabic prosody, a discussion that combined practice and theory and that dealt not only with verse technique, but also with ways in which it has developed within, and been affected by, our larger literary and intellectual history.

I recently spoke with a prominent young poet who didn't get any metrical training in high school, university, or in her MFA program. It seems a whole generation has grown up thinking of poetry as self-expression – or worse yet, therapy – and have very little insight into what makes the great poems of the past work, technically speaking. I've noticed that even some 'important' poets and critics can't scan.

A few years back, an issue of *Poets & Writers* carried an interview of a poet, in which the interviewer asks the poet if her poems scan. That a writer with an apparent background in poetry, working for a publication devoted to poets and fiction writers, can't tell whether a poem scans says a lot about the current state of metrical understanding – or misunderstanding.

I've also noticed that poetry critics – even in eminent journals – refer to verse as 'formal' when it may simply have the same number of lines in each stanza.

In some instances, the critic or poet may be motivated by a well-intentioned wish to address prosodic issues, but may lack the knowledge to discuss or recognize metrical features of poems. In other cases, the critic or poet may be motivated by a less well-intentioned desire to appear to be technically responsible or sophisticated, without actually having to learn about, let alone embrace metrics. And yet other writers almost seem to be motivated by a perverse desire to mislead – to undermine so-called formal poetry by identifying it with poems and procedures that have little or nothing to do with the traditional versification.

With the last two groups, you are usually treated to a terminological bait-and-switch operation. At one moment, 'form' appears to be a synonym for 'metre', and at the next moment, 'form' is serving to validate or commend elements of writing totally unrelated to metrical organization.

It's perfectly okay to discuss 'form' in a broadly aesthetic or philosophic manner. That's not the problem. The problem is using the term to confuse rather than illuminate the nature of traditional verse practice.

Regardless of your reservations, you've been associated with the 'movement' called 'New Formalism'. Some claim that it is an invention of the New Formalists that obloquy was heaped on metrical verse twenty or thirty years ago – at least in America.

One doesn't want to sound querulous, but the obloquy was real and widespread. When I was a student, most poets seemed to regard metre as, in Robert Bly's characterization, a 'jail'. Incidentally, this attitude was not limited to the United States. The fifth edition of *The Oxford Companion to English Literature* concludes its entry for 'metre' by saying, 'Verse in the 20th century has largely escaped the straitjacket of traditional metrics.' And no sooner did metre start to come back in the late 1980s than various parties started launching salvos at it. There was a long cover story in *American Poetry Review* entitled 'Neo-Formalism: A Dangerous Nostalgia', in which the author accused metrical poets of 'cultural imperialism'.

I remember: the 1990 article accused the poets of having a 'social as well as a linguistic agenda'. Another critic called Neo-Formalists 'the Reaganites of poetry'. Even a recent issue of the American Poetry Review *made a dismissive reference to 'neo-conservative formalism'.*

Apparently, many poets in the United States feel that metre is elitist and anti-democratic. In Missing Measures, *you cite Robert Bly's statement, 'As Whitman saw, the rhymed metred poem is, in our consciousness, so tied to the feudal stratified society of England that such a metred poem refuses to merge well with the content of American experience. We therefore have no choice but to write free verse.'*

That argument – that metrical forms are products of feudal or aristocratic Europe and are inappropriate to American democracy – is ubiquitous. One of our recent poet laureates described accentual-syllabics as 'the principal way in which the educated classes in Europe mystified their utterance and gave it repressive authority, which they called poetry.' And our first laureate of the new millennium begins a 21-line free-verse poem entitled 'American Sonnet', 'We do not speak like Petrarch or wear a hat like Spenser.' He has another loosey-goosey sonnet that says of writing sonnets, 'How easily it goes unless you get Elizabethan / and insist the iambic bongos must be played / and rhymes positioned at the ends of lines.'

All poets should be free to adopt whatever styles or modes they wish to, and no one should try to restrict anyone else's range of expression. But you'd think that our leading bards had never heard of Robert Burns, listened to folk music, or read metrical verse by impecunious writers like Keats and Robinson, or a sonnet by a Harlem Renaissance writer like Claude McKay.

That misperception accounts for some of the bizarre hostility that Missing Measures *excited. My favourite story of course is about the anonymous phone call.*

That was bizarre. The phone rang one afternoon, and when I picked up, this gruff voice asked if I was Timothy Steele the poet. Upon my saying, yes, he called me an s.o.b and told me that American poetry came from Whitman, and I'd better wise up. Then the line went dead. As I think I once said to you, when I set the receiver back down in its cradle, I thought, 'Gee, there really is a Poetry Mafia!'

For safety's sake, I should publicly say here that I'm not out to grab any action from the Poe-Whitman syndicate of American Literature. And though I sometimes run with toughs in the Dickinson-Hawthorne-Melville family, we have *never* distributed copies of *Missing Measures* in Vegas, Atlantic City or any other territory where they might give offence. Contrary to the word on the street, I know my place.

Will metre ever hold the sway it once did?

It's returned significantly already; it's more of a part of poetry today than it was twenty-five years ago. But whether metre will ever again be central to poetic practice at large is another question. Some poets will always be drawn to it, for its challenges and pleasures and for the appeal it makes to the ear and memory. Intelligent free verse poets will encourage it, knowing that keeping metre alive will benefit the experimental tradition and contribute to a healthy diversity of practice. But more factors are against a general metrical revival than are for it.

For example?

So many poets in recent decades have put all their eggs in the free verse basket: it is only natural that few of them want a change. Henri Coulette once related that a much-belaurelled poet-friend of his had remarked, 'If meter comes back, I'll be out of business.' And, make no mistake, poetry is a business for many poets today, a business involving hefty grants and prizes, and university positions with six-figure salaries.

A related problem is the technical temptation of free verse. It's easier to write passably in free verse than in metre. Please note that I say 'passably' rather than 'excellently'. In the theoretical sense of creating, without metre, something possessing a high and appealing degree of rhythmical organization, nothing is harder than free verse. But when one is beginning, it takes time, patience, and practice to master traditional versification and to learn to write in a personal and idiomatically fluent manner in metre, rhyme, and stanza. It also can be daunting. If you undertake a conventional sonnet or poems in couplets the attempt will immediately call to mind – and invite comparison with – the great sonnets of Shakespeare and Keats, or the couplets of Chaucer, Pope, and Browning. When you write traditional verse, you're playing with the big boys and girls; if your game isn't up to snuff, they'll blast you off the court in a second.

Certainly your preferences almost caused Louisiana State University Press to turn down your first book, Uncertainties and Rest.

An anonymous outside reader of the book asked at the end of his or her report, 'Does the press want on its list at this time a collection that is characteristically witty, formal, sophisticated?'

They showed that to you?

Yes, they were undecided whether to take the book, and asked me to respond to the criticism. I said that it sounded as if the reader were recommending that the press stick to collections that were dull, haphazard, and primitive. Beverly Jarrett, the acquisitions editor, thought that this was amusing, and they gave me the benefit of the doubt and went ahead with the collection. A second and more enthusiastic report had been written by Richard Eberhart, so there was some additional support there.

How do you write? How often do you write? What circumstances encourage your best poetry?

I write whenever I have the chance. I write most happily early in the morning, in long hand, in pen or pencil, in so-called exercise or composition books – those notebooks with black-and-white cardboard covers and blue-lined pages and red-lined margins. Using these notebooks means I don't lose drafts – they stay there in the notebook so that I can return to them if subsequent revisions take me down a blind alley. In addition, the notebooks let me doodle idly when the Muse wanders away somewhere. When a stanza or poem is more or less complete, I'll type it on the computer.

You never compose on the computer – not even prose?

I love my Mac; it makes my life much easier than it would be otherwise. I do much of my correspondence now directly on the computer. But I grew up writing long hand, and didn't even own a typewriter until I received an Olivetti portable as a high school graduation present. So I find the computer more valuable for storing and shifting blocks of text (and now for Internet access) than for fundamental composition. And so far as the writing of verse is concerned, the computer as a physical object has – at least for me – the same disadvantage that the typewriter does. It reproaches you for inactivity. It seems to beg you to tap in material when, much of the time, your task is to sit and think patiently, silently weighing a phrase or an idea.

You've produced three slim volumes of poetry since 1979 – four, counting your collected, Sapphics and Uncertainties. *It's not hard to find poets who have six times that output. Some say the pressure to impress university tenure committees is pushing poets to produce poetry like scholarly articles – to the detriment of poetry, inevitably. Do you feel poets are under too much pressure today to 'produce'? How do you resist that pressure?*

Publish or perish has been bad for scholarship – it's resulted in the publication of many unnecessary, unhelpful essays and books – and it's bad for poetry. I remember how stunned I was when I heard a poet say he was rushing out another collection of poems to obtain a promotion at his school. What a reason to write verse!

As for my situation, Cal State has historically aimed at providing good solid undergraduate education. Most of us on the English Department faculty are generalists. Our primary obligation is to teach a broad range of literature courses to our students. I've never been hassled to write more. And if I ever had been pressured to crank out verse for pragmatic rather than poetic reasons, I'd like to think that I would simply have told the pressurizers to take a hike.

In 'Baker Beach at Sunset' you write 'and, yes, I know / I've written nothing in three months.' Vikram Seth churned out the remarkable The Golden Gate *in thirteen months, averaging, by my reckoning, over six-hundred lines of verse a month. Doesn't that make you just want to die? Perhaps I'm speaking for myself! I certainly envy that enormous facility.*

Such facility is wonderful, and The Golden Gate is a great achievement. As Vikram himself would observe, however, that poem is a special case. It is a genuine old-fashioned (in the best sense) novel in verse. Once under sail, a project like that takes on a life and momentum of its own. Writing one poem of three-hundred pages, and writing three-hundred one-page poems, are different things.

There is perhaps another question here. Do certain poets, such as Hardy, need to write quite a few not-so-good poems to produce their masterworks? That may well be true, though when it happens, such poets have to count on the patience of their readers (or the taste of an editor distilling their work down into a Selected volume) to distinguish the better from the worse.

Daniel Mendelsohn, discussing some of the New Formalist poets, wrote in the New York Review of Books*: 'But if the forms these young poets embraced were classical, the content was anything but Olympian. What distinguished the "New" Formalists from the academic formalists of the previous generation – that is, from the poets influenced by the New Criticism – was their rejection of ironic personae, literary allusiveness, and abstruse diction and syntax in favor of vigorous colloquial speech and everyday subject matter.' Let's talk about that 'everyday subject matter' a bit.*

Wordsworth, in his preface to Lyrical Ballads, speaks of his interest in treating incidents and situations from real life and throwing over them the colors of imagination. And my aspirations run in the direction more of Wordsworth than of Coleridge, whose concern was to see to what extent he could familiarize supernaturalistic subject matter.

You have described your poetry as taking place at the 'intersection of nature and human nature'. I've noticed that your poetry often circles the quotidian moments – a Latina girl riding a bike through a West Los Angeles neighbourhood in 'Near Olympic', a cat on the patio in 'Faustina', doing the after-dinner wash-up in 'Sapphics Against Anger'. Any philosophy behind these choices?

Too often we ask life for things it can't give us, and ignore ungratefully the things it can. One benefit of the literary arts is that they encourage us to see the world around us more truly, sharply, and appreciatively than we usually do.

A common complaint made about formalists is that they have focused on form at the expense of subject. While I think few would argue that the craftsmanship of poetry could use a good brushing-up after the twentieth century – if not a rehaul – it's not what we memorize a poem for.

Every fine poem has an emotional charge or is informed by intellectual zest or conviction. It's a poor poem that merely illustrates the rules of its composition.

Kant divided the faculties of mind, separating Truth (science and metaphysics), the Good and the Useful (ethics), and Beauty (aesthetics and teleology) – and you have argued that in doing so he provided a justification for separating poetry from metaphysical and ethical concerns – hence many of the shortcomings we see in poetry today, no?

Yes, but in defence of Kant and others – like Coleridge – in that tradition of idealist aesthetics, they recognized the dangers of that division.

To practice fruitfully an art or science, we need to be able examine different aspects of reality on their own terms, while at the same time remaining sensitive to the connections between the aspects and to the ways in which they intersect. Science must be at liberty to study the material universe in a pure and dispassionate manner: it is foolish and counter-productive to let the moralist sit at the scientist's shoulder and, with a view to religious beliefs or political agendas, approve or veto insights and discoveries. Yet it is just as foolish not to consider the possible ethical and aesthetic impact of our science: as critical as it is to encourage and support free and adventurous scientific research, the products of it must be evaluated in light of ethics and aesthetics, or we're likely to end up with nothing more than a lot of fancy weapons and a very polluted planet.

Similarly, most of us feel that art and artists should be autonomous, in the sense that art has its own ways of getting at and illuminating reality and it does this best when we allow the artist the greatest possible independence of mind. Yet, at the same time, we know the goofy things that can happen to art when it divorces itself from scientific rigour and from the moral, social, and political concerns of its audience.

Does this account, at least partially, for why 'eccentricity and obscurity are qualities we have long grown accustomed to expect of poets'? You wrote that over two decades ago – I take it you still feel it is true?

This is another matter that concerns the romantic period and that philosophical-aesthetic tradition represented in Kant and Coleridge. As many people have observed, the eighteenth century was a watershed in the history of the arts. We've admired and have tried to develop the valuable parts of the romantic legacy – its spirit of free-ranging inquiry, for instance, and its passionate concern for individual liberty. But we've never quite recovered our balance after the romantic tilt to subjectivity. In one sense, the free-verse movement is not really 'modern' but 'romantic'. Romantic subjectivism is given an additional turn of the screw, and the screw is applied to prosodic technique. Yeats perceived this very shrewdly when he commented, in his 'Modern Poetry' essay, that Eliot was the most revolutionary man in poetry during his lifetime, but that 'his revolution was stylistic alone.'

Frequently, people say that art swings like a pendulum back and forth between periods of freedom and periods of restraint, but this is a misleading analogy in terms of the last two-hundred-and-fifty years. Though the pendulum has been swinging, it's as if the mechanism has become damaged. Instead of swinging in a full arc of a hundred and eighty degrees, it's got stuck; it's been oscillating in an ever-smaller arc, high up and exclusively on the freedom side. It has been quite a while since it's fallen to plumb, much less swung a ways back up on the side of classical restraint.

Do you think that the self-absorption evident in much recent English-language poetry may account for some of the popularity of Eastern European poets in the 1970s and 1980s – Czeslaw Milosz comes to mind – who were still working out religious, ethical, and metaphysical questions in their works?

Yes, Anna Akhmatova and Osip Mandelstam are other cases in point. Terrible historical circumstances – the harrowing conditions of living under the modern ideological state and witnessing tyranny and genocide

– forced them to remain focused on fundamental issues, and that gives their work tremendous power. The same is true with, say, Käthe Kollwitz's lithographs and woodcuts.

Ideally, however, we shouldn't need crises to keep us grounded in reality. If we're to survive as a species, we must in the future exercise more foresight and intelligence than we have in the past.

Let me build my own argument against the contention that contemporary American poets aren't concerned with social and religious themes. Among many examples I could choose, the final lines of your 'Pacific Rim':

> ... A brutal century
> Draws to a close. Bewildering genetrix,
> As your miraculous experiment
> In consciousness hangs in the balance, do
> You pity those enacting it? The headlands'
> Blunt contours sloping to the oceanside,
> Do angels weep for our folly? Merciful,
> Do you accompany our mortality
> Just as, low to the water, the pelican
> Swiftly pursues his shadow down a swell?

Well, this seems pretty Olympian to me. In fact, Mendelsohn himself describes your 'coolly delicate, sometimes elaborately argued lyrics that recall the metaphysical poets' – a group hardly confined to 'everyday subject matter'.

We all want to develop a style that suits us and is authentically our own, without becoming a prisoner of it. It's important to be distinctive, but we always should try to write better and expand our range in tone, in thought, in feeling, and in subject. And though my preference has always been to write as naturally as possible and to write about the world around me, I have the greatest respect for passionately sublime writers like Milton and Hopkins. And I hope – this may be a vain hope – to be able at times to reach for something like the sublime myself.

You decry fashionable emotions, and perhaps a few more tenacious ones as well. In 'Baker Beach at Sunset', you write:

> But I've learned what too much self-scrutiny

> *Does to the spirit. Secondhand beliefs,*
> *The palpitating soul: how carefully*
> *We shelter and array these.*

In 'Sapphics against Anger' you write that 'melancholy is a sin, though / Stylish at present.'

There are fashions in emotions no less than in clothes and movies, and we should be as sceptical of these as we are of the other fashions. They aren't real and intrinsic to us, and if we let them into our lives, they can supplant what is real and intrinsic. I maybe should add, with regard to both those poems, that the explicitly stated – and real – object of criticism is me. 'Baker Beach' was written in the summer of 1976 and 'Sapphics' in late 1981 or early 1982. Those poems have sometimes been read as aesthetic manifestos, but they weren't written in that spirit at all. They grew out of self-disappointment and the hope I might in the future overcome my tendencies to despondency and impatience.

Despondency and impatience! That would be a surprise to so many who have commended your equanimity. Many have commented about your even-tempered character – but do I detect a note of peevishness in a few of your epigrams, like 'Pal'?

It's cheering to hear that I have a reputation for even-temperedness, though it is quite undeserved. As my wife will assure you, I'm really just another neurotic writer. As for 'Pal', I didn't intend to be peevish; but epigrams are a form of satire, and, in satirical verse, one is usually expressing distaste for certain kinds of conduct. The trick is to satirize the sin and not the sinner. If epigrams are personal and specific, and not in some way comprehensive, they can seem merely cruel jokes at someone's expense.

I can't help noticing a trend toward the classical virtues in your verse – restraint, moderation, modesty, equanimity – perhaps in keeping with your classical forms. In 'Hortulus' you note 'Too great an ardor is a common blunder' and urge a bird to 'Woo clemently' and, more poignantly,

> *the sad mirth serving those who gauge*
>
> *The gap between the longed-for and the real,*
> *Who grasp provisional joy, who must not be*

> *Desolate, however desolate they feel.*

'Hortulus' is partly about romance. When we're in love, we're often so concerned with our longings and anxieties that we forget about the other person's feelings. 'Dependent Nature' is a little darker and tries to suggest that we should resist, whenever it's humanly possible, discouragements. We have to keep going. Though we should never shut our hearts against the suffering and losses of life, we also have to try to be thoughtful and cheerful, if for no other reason than to give others support and comfort.

From Daniel Mendelsohn again: 'Timothy Steele has done much to give back structural stability to (it sometimes seems) love itself as well as to love poetry, sagely rejecting excesses of passion, both poetic and emotional, in favour of the comforts of form.' In 'Love Poem' you write:

> That evil is the formless and unspoken,
> And that peace rests in form and nomenclature.

Comment?

It is by articulating our experience that we understand its significance. Becoming articulate allows us to interact with others and allows them to interact with and understand us. One reason we love novels, plays, and poems is that their narratives illuminate our lives and enable us to enrich them and connect them with other lives.

You've often been compared with Richard Wilbur. Is he a hard act to live up to and follow? He's a personal friend – how did you meet?

Dick is a national treasure, and to be compared with him is very flattering. He's not only one of the greats of American poetry, but is, with Chaucer, Dryden, and Pope, one of the top poet-translators in our language. He has excelled over as long a haul as anyone in our national literature, including Henry James. Nearly sixty years separate his recent *Collected Poems* from his stunning inaugural collection, *The Beautiful Changes*. And many of the relatively new poems – 'For C.', 'This Pleasing Anxious Being', 'Zea', 'A Barred Owl', 'The Reader', and 'Man Running'– are among his very best. With others of my generation, I've been reading him since student days, and such poems as 'Year's End', 'The Pardon', 'An Event', 'A Baroque Wall-Fountain in the Villa Sciarra', and 'Love Calls Us to the Things of This World' have long been part of the texture of our experience –

Don't forget his title poem, 'Mayflies', which is unforgettable and exquisite.

Yes, indeed. Dick has also given us the opportunity to watch the transformations of a master poet. We've seen him evolve into a style that is more direct than his virtuosic, earlier manner, but that nevertheless retains all his talent for the surprisingly right word and for the illuminating metaphor.
 I believe our correspondence – mostly by postcard – dates back to the late 1970s. We did not meet until 1987 when he kindly invited me to read at the Library of Congress during his laureateship.

In 1995, you said it was too early to know if New Formalism would have a lasting effect on the American poetry scene. Is it still too early to offer even a preliminary assessment?

It's still pretty early to tell, but, as we noted a while ago, metre has come back significantly. And perhaps the hostility towards the movement speaks of its strength and ultimate significance.

I've noticed a tendency for the more successful New Formalists to distance themselves from 'New Formalism'. Of course, no one wants to be ghettoized or pigeonholed. On the other hand, it's troubling when your children become successful, and are suddenly embarrassed at being associated with you.

In defence of those New Formalists who, at one time or another, cringed at being named thus – and this probably includes every New Formalist – it should be stressed that the movement was not self-generated. It wasn't invented and announced in the way that, for instance, Pound and Flint invented and announced Imagism or in the way that Hans Arp, Hugo Ball, Richard Huelsenbeck, and Tristan Tzara invented and announced Dada. 'New Formalism' was something that people suspicious of metre invented as a label of opprobrium. I wrote and published metred verse for more than fifteen years before there was New Formalism, and it was dispiriting, when people finally started to notice the work, to have that tag fixed to my forehead. In the same way, it was bemusing, when *Missing Measures* was published, to see it treated as if it were a New Formalist discussion of contemporary verse, when the book was written prior to New Formalism, focused on poetry of the late nineteenth and early twentieth century, and never even mentioned the term 'New Formalism'.

Even when critics apply the term in a positive, praising manner, one sometimes feels embarrassed. It suggests that some of us are to be credited with saving metre, rhyme, and stanza, whereas the real heroes and heroines are those poets of the preceding generation, such as Bowers, Hecht, Kennedy, Pinkerton, and Wilbur, who continued to defend and develop traditional verse when almost everyone else had gone over to vers libre.

In a lighter vein, a few of them have called themselves 'Paleo-Formalists'.

That's nicely put and brings up another point. The only real New Formalist in English is Geoffrey Chaucer. What's new about the New Formalism is what's new about the new poetry of any age. Poets are addressing issues of their time, and are grappling with current developments and ideas.

Having said all this, I'm happy to be associated with other metrical poets of my generation and with all those who have shown fellow feeling, good will, and camaraderie in the art of verse.

I believe Samuel Johnson was concurring with the Romans when he said, 'Courage is reckoned the greatest of all virtues; because, unless a man has that virtue, he has no security for preserving any other.' Certainly I think your career as poet, critic, and scholar exhibits significant intellectual courage and integrity, though not, perhaps, of the headline-grabbing variety. May I quote from your 'Decisions, Decisions'?

> The contingent spirit must whistle in the dark,
> Bucking itself up, choosing, choosing, knowing
> That time may claim those choices with its own
> Inevitable air of history.

Is that a critical role of poetry for you?

Poetry has many functions, not the least of which is to elevate and comfort people. This doesn't mean that poetry should always endeavor to be optimistic. The writer who can look courageously and honestly at life at its worst can strengthen us no less than the author who illuminates positive elements of experience. But one touchstone for me has been the letter that Haydn addressed, late in life, to a small choral society that had written to tell him how much they had enjoyed performing his *Creation* oratorio. 'You give me the welcome assurance – and this is the greatest comfort of my declining years – that I am often the source from which you, and many other families receptive to heartfelt emotion, derive pleasure and satisfaction in the quiet of your homes. How soothing this reflection is to me! Often, as I struggled with obstacles of every kind opposed to my works – often, as my physical and mental powers sank, and I had difficulty keeping to my chosen course – an inner voice whispered to me: "There are so few happy and contented people here below – on every hand care and sorrow pursue them – perhaps your work may someday be a source from which men and women laden with anxieties and burdened with affairs may derive a few moments of rest and refreshment." This, then, was a powerful motive to persevere, this the reason why I can even now look back with profound satisfaction on what I have accomplished in my art through uninterrupted effort and application over a long succession of years.'

SELECT BIBLIOGRAPHIES

COMPILED BY RYAN ROBERTS

(i) Dick Davis

Poetry

Books

In the Distance (Anvil Press, London, 1975).
Seeing the World (Anvil Press, London, 1980; Reprinted 1984).
The Covenant: Poems 1979-1983 (Anvil Press, London, 1984).
Devices and Desires: New and Selected Poems, 1967-1987 (Anvil Press, London, 1989).
A Kind of Love: Selected and New Poems (Arkansas University Press, 1991) [A revised and expanded edition of preceding book, including a short section of verse translations from Persian].
Touchwood: Poems 1991-1994 (Anvil Press, London, 1996).
Belonging: Poems (Swallow Press/Ohio University Press, 2002; Anvil Press, London, 2002).
A Trick of Sunlight: Poems (Swallow Press/Ohio University Press, 2006).

Chapbooks, Limited Editions, Broadsides, and Similar Publications

Visitations: 6 Poems (Ampersand Press, Colchester, UK, 1983) [Limited to 200 copies; Emanations, no. 4].
What the Mind Wants (Robert L. Barth, Florence, KY, 1984) [Limited to 200 copies].
"Baucis and Philemon" (Aralia Press, West Chester, PA, October 1984) [Limited edition of 50 copies printed on dark green paper; The first sonnet from the poet's *Four Visitations*].
Four Visitations (Aralia Press, West Chester, PA, 1985) [Limited to 240 copies].
Lares: Poems 1985-1986 (Sea Cliff Press, New York / Cummington Press, Omaha, 1986) [Limited to 300 copies bound in gray paper wrappers, handsewn].
Heresy (Santa Barbara, CA, 1988).
Let Them be Changed: Poems from the Persian (Robert L. Barth, Florence, KY, 1989) [Limited to 200 copies].
Borrowed Ware: Epigrams from Medieval Persian, 9th to 13th Centuries (Robert L. Barth, Florence, KY, 1990) [Limited to 200 copies, of which 25 are signed and lettered A-AA by the author, bound in white covers with an additional poem in holograph by the author. The remaining 175 copies are numbered and signed by the author].
Middle Age (Robert L. Barth, Florence, KY, 1990) [Broadside, 11 x 14 cm; Postcard Series, no. 2].
A Sasanian Palace (The Turret Bookshop, London, 1992) [Broadside, 30 x 21 cm].
Just a Small One (Robert L. Barth, Florence, KY, 2000) [Limited to 125 copies; 25 copies are signed and include a holograph poem].
A Monorhyme for the Shower (Aralia Press, West Chester, PA, 2001) [Broadside, 19 x 30

cm; Limited to 150 copies].

Translations

The Conference of the Birds, with Afkham Darbandi (Penguin Books, London 1984) [Verse translation from the Persian into heroic couplets of *Mantiq al-tayr*, by Farid ud-Din Attar].

The Little Virtues (Carcanet Press, Manchester, 1985 / Seaver Books, New York, 1986) [Translation of *Le Piccole Virtu*, from the Italian of Natalia Ginzburg].

The City and The House (Carcanet Press, Manchester 1986 / Seaver Books, New York, 1987) [Translation of *La Citta e La Casa*, from the Italian of Natalia Ginzburg].

The Legend of Seyavash (Penguin Classics, London, 1992; Reprinted 1994) [Verse translation of a book-length section of the *Shahnameh* of Ferdowsi; Introduction, translation and notes by DD].

My Uncle Napoleon, by Iraj Pezeshkzad (Mage, Washington, DC, 1996) [Translation of what is, in Iran, the best known and most popular Iranian novel; a comic novel dealing among many other things with the invasion of Iran by the Allies in World War II].

Borrowed Ware: Epigrams from Medieval Persian, 9th to 13th Centuries (Robert L. Barth, Florence, KY, 1990) [Limited to 200 copies, of which 25 are signed and lettered A-AA by the author, bound in white covers with an additional poem in holograph by the author. The remaining 175 copies are numbered and signed by the author].

Borrowed Ware: Medieval Persian Epigrams (Anvil Press, London, 1996) [Translations of *c.*150 Medieval Persian poems (*c.*950-*c.*1600), with an extensive introduction and notes on individual poets].

Borrowed Ware: Medieval Persian Epigrams [expanded, bilingual edition] (Mage, Washington, DC, 1997).

Let Them be Changed: Poems from the Persian (Robert L. Barth, Florence, KY, 1989) [Limited to 200 copies].

The Lion and the Throne (Mage, Washington, DC, 1997) [First in a projected three-volume series to include in translation all the major narratives of Ferdowsi's *Shahnameh*].

Fathers and Sons: Stories from the Shahnameh of Ferdowsi, Volume II (Mage, Washington, DC, 2000).

Sunset of Empire: Stories from the Shahnameh of Ferdowsi, Volume III (Mage, Washington, DC, 2004).

The Shahnameh of Ferdowsi (Viking, New York / Penguin, London, 2006) [Complete three-volume translation of the Persian epic, with new introduction and some revisions of the work originally published by Mage].

Editions Works or Selections

Selected Writings of Thomas Traherne (Carcanet Press, Manchester, 1980; Reprinted 1988).

New Writing from the North, with David Williams (Mid Northumberland Arts Group, Ashington, Northumberland, 1988).

The Rubáiyát of Omar Khayyám, translated by Edward FitzGerald, with introduction, notes, appendices and glossary by DD (Penguin Books, London, 1989).

Prose

Books

Wisdom and Wilderness: The Achievement of Yvor Winters (University of Georgia Press, Athens GA, 1983).

Epic and Sedition: the Case of Ferdowsi's Shahnameh (University of Arkansas Press, Fayetteville, 1992; Mage, Washington, DC, 1999).

Panthea's Children: Hellenistic Novels and Medieval Persian Romances (Bibliotheca Persica, New York, 2002).

(ii) Rachel Hadas

Poetry

Books

Starting from Troy (D.R. Godine, Boston, 1975) [Godine poetry chapbook, second series].
Slow Transparency (Wesleyan University Press, Middletown, CT, 1983).
A Son from Sleep (Wesleyan University Press, Middletown, CT, 1987).
Pass It On (Princeton University Press, Princeton, 1989).
Unending Dialogue: Voices from an AIDS Poetry Workshop (Faber and Faber, Boston, 1991) [Contains 16 poems by RH].
Mirrors of Astonishment (Rutgers University Press, New Brunswick, 1992).
The Empty Bed (Wesleyan University Press / University Press of New England, Hanover, NH, 1995).
Halfway down the Hall: New and Selected Poems (Wesleyan University Press, Middletown, CT / University Press of New England, Hanover, NH, 1998).
Indelible (Wesleyan University Press, Middletown, CT, 2001).
Laws: Poems (Zoo Press, Lincoln, NE, 2004).
The River of Forgetfulness (David Robert Books, Cincinnati, OH, 2006).

Chapbooks, Limited Editions, Broadsides, and Similar Publications

Night Drive (Sackbut Press, Milwaukee, WI, 1981) [Broadside, 11 x 17 cm; Postcard Series].
Two Poems (Dim Gray Bar Press, New York, 2000) [Limited to 100 signed copies].

Translations

Xenos, Stephanos, *Trelles* (Athena, 1978) [translated and with an afterword by RH].
Other Worlds Than This: Translations (Rutgers University Press, New Brunswick, 1994) [Tibullus, Seneca, Victor Hugo, Baudelaire, Mallarme, Rimbaud, LaForgue, Valéry, and Karyota].
Seneca, *Oedipus the King* (Johns Hopkins University Press, 1994) [Roman Drama Series].
Euripides, *Helen* (University of Pennsylvania Press, 1997) [Greek Drama Series].

Prose

Books

Form, Cycle, Infinity: Landscape Imagery in the Poetry of Robert Frost and George Seferis (Bucknell University Press, Lewisburg, 1985).

Living in Time (Rutgers University Press, New Brunswick, 1990).
The Double Legacy: Reflections on a Pair of Deaths (Faber and Faber, Boston, 1995).
Merrill, Cavafy, Poems, and Dreams (University of Michigan Press, Ann Arbor, 2000) [Poets on Poetry Series].

Forthcoming

Classics (selected prose), (David Robert Books, Cincinnati, OH)

Short Fiction

'Classics', *New England Review*, 22:2, Spring 2001: 36+.

Edited Works or Selections

Saturday's Women: Eileen W. Barnes Award Anthology, edited with Charlotte Mandel and Maxine Silverman (Saturday Press, Upper Montclair, NJ, 1982).
Unending Dialogue: Voices from an AIDS Poetry Workshop (Faber and Faber, Boston, 1991).
Phillips, Carl, *In the Blood* (Northeastern University Press, Boston, 1992) [selected and introduced by RH].

(iii) Timothy Steele

Poetry

Books

Uncertainties and Rest (Louisiana State University Press, Baton Rouge, 1979).
Sapphics Against Anger and Other Poems (Random House, New York, 1986).
The Color Wheel (Johns Hopkins University Press, Baltimore, 1994).
Sapphics and Uncertainties: Poems 1970-1986 (University of Arkansas Press, Fayetteville, 1995).
Toward the Winter Solstice and Other Poems (Swallow Press/Ohio University Press, Athens, Ohio, 2006).

Chapbooks, Limited Editions, Broadsides, and Similar Publications

'Waiting for the Storm' [broadside] (Horn Press, Los Angeles, 1977).
A Diatribe to Dr Steele [with Charles B. Gullans] (Symposium Press/Amaranth Press, Los Angeles, 1982) [Limited to 300 signed copies, of which 25 are lettered A to AA and 275 are numbered].
'In Memory of Andy Horn' [broadside] ([California], May 1983) [Memorial poem for Andrew H. Horn, dean of UCLA Library School].
The Prudent Heart (Symposium Press, Los Angeles, 1983).
Nine Poems (Robert L. Barth, Florence, KY, 1984) [Limited to 150 signed copies, of which 25 are lettered A to AA and 125 are numbered].
On Harmony (Abattoir Editions, Omaha, 1984).
Short Subjects (Robert L. Barth, Florence, KY, 1985).
Beatitudes (Words Press, Child Okeford, Dorset, 1988).
Jerusalem Delivered [broadside] (Robert L. Barth, Florence, KY, 1990).
'In Passing', [broadside published by Bernard Stone and Raymond Danowski] (The Turret Bookshop, London, July 1992).
'For Victoria, Traveling in Europe', [broadside with an illustration by Abraham Brewster] (The Oliphant Press, New York, October 1996) [For the Friends of the Amherst College Library].
'For Peter Brier, on His Retirement from California State University, Los Angeles' [Poem printed in the programme for the retirement celebration for Professor Peter A. Brier, 6 November 1998].
'Birds in Spring' [Poem printed in the program for the annual Fletcher Lecture at Nicholls State University, delivered by the author on Thursday, 22 March 2001 at the Talbot Theater, Nicholls State University, Thibodaux, Louisiana].
Starr Farm Beach (Aralia Press, West Chester, PA, 2005).

Edited Works or Selections

The Music of His History: Poems for Charles Gullans on His Sixtieth Birthday, edited by Timothy Steele (Robert L. Barth Press, Florence, KY, 1989).
The Poems of J. V. Cunningham, edited with an introduction and commentary by Timothy

Steele (Swallow Press/Ohio University Press, Athens, OH, 1997).

Robert Herrick: 10 Epigrams [Epigrammatist Postcard Series, no. 5] (Robert L. Barth Press, Edgewood, KY, 1997) [Selected by TS, with additions].

Prose

Books

Missing Measures: Modern Poetry and the Revolt Against Meter (University of Arkansas Press, Fayetteville, 1990).

All the Fun's in How You Say a Thing: An Explanation of Meter and Versification (Ohio University Press, Athens, OH, 1999).

Three Poets

in conversation

Dick Davis
Rachel Hadas
Timothy Steele